Painting Pets on Rocks

LIN WELLFORD

NORTH LIGHT BOOKS
CINCINNATI, OHIO

ABOUT THE AUTHOR

After a childhood in Florida, living in the Arkansas Ozarks gave Lin Wellford a true appreciation for all the wonderful rocks and stones that line creek beds, beaches and country roads all over the world. She developed a missionary's zeal for spreading the word that rock painting is not only an inexpensive and exciting art form, but also a fabulous tool for helping people discover and connect with their own creative natures.

"It's a thrill to hear from people who are delighted and amazed that they were able to turn ordinary rocks into works of art," Lin explains. "But when someone tells me that she now sees herself as an artist, I know that a far more magical transformation has taken place."

The popularity of her "rock books" has been a pleasant surprise, leading to television appearances and other opportunities to spread the word about rocks as a fabulous art material for people of all ages and abilities.

The mother of three grown daughters, Lin continues to paint, write and collect rocks in Green Forest, Arkansas, her adopted hometown.

04   03   02   01   00   5   4   3   2   1

Library of Congress Cataloging-in-Publication Data

Wellford, Lin.
    Painting pets on rocks / by Lin Wellford
        p.   cm.
    Includes index.
    ISBN 1-58180-032-0 (alk. paper)
    1. Stone painting. 2. Animals in art. I. Title
TT370 .W466 2000   00-035507
751.4'26--dc21   CIP

Editors: Nicole R. Klungle and Jane Friedman
Designer: Sandy Kent
Production artists: Kathy Bergstrom and Kathy Gardner
Production coordinator: Emily Gross

DEDICATION

For my husband of the past quarter century, Klaus Kupfersberger.

Let's go for the gold!

Table *of* Contents

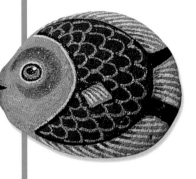

EXOTIC ANIMALS

CATS

Painting Pets on Rocks

Introduction

Whether furry, feathered or finned, the animals we choose to live with occupy a special place in our hearts as well as our homes. Capturing the likeness of a beloved pet on a rock is a wonderful way to celebrate that special bond, while creating a lasting remembrance.

Ever since my first book, *The Art of Painting Animals on Rocks*, was published in 1994, letters have arrived from new rock painters all over the world. Many people wrote just to express their excitement at discovering this unique art form. Some wanted me to know they had never painted anything that pleased them before trying rock painting. Others confessed to being so intimidated by art that they hadn't even picked up a paint brush since childhood. But the idea of turning an ordinary rock into a three-dimensional piece of art was simply irresistible, and in the process of painting they uncovered talents they never dreamed they possessed. Even accomplished artists have found

that painting on rocks is a way to create wonderful, freestanding pieces that never need matting or framing.

There's no magic to it (although turning rocks into art does seem almost like some mysterious form of alchemy). Painting on a surface that already has shape simply provides a shortcut to achieving realistic results. The fact that rocks are three-dimensional objects means you can paint without worrying about perspective, backgrounds, foregrounds and many other aspects of painting that often confuse and frustrate novice artists. People of all ages have discovered that painting on rocks makes it easier to get realistic results that amaze themselves and others. One painted rock will usually lead to another and another.

An added advantage to rock painting is that it is not possible to ruin a rock. If you aren't happy with your first attempt, simply paint it over and try again. If you decide that the rock you chose was not the right shape after all, it can always go back to

being a rock until you think of some other subject for which it may be better suited.

When I was painting my very first rocks, there weren't any other painted rocks I could compare mine to, so I was thrilled with my results, crude as those early efforts were. Your very first rock will not likely be the very best you'll ever do. If it were, there would be little incentive to ever paint a second one. The satisfaction of seeing progress as you gain skills and experience is another rewarding aspect of this unique and exciting art form.

Because of its low-cost, rock painting is perfect for group activities with people of all ages. Scout groups, nursing homes, day camps and school art teachers have all found rock painting to be a great recreational activity. Disabled and handicapped people have also discovered that this can be a satisfying and rewarding—yet affordable—hobby.

So what are you waiting for? Pick up a brush and get rockin'!

Getting Started

The popularity of rock painting is relatively new, but painting on rocks is surely among the oldest of all art forms. In the Stone Age, primitive humans mixed their own pigments and painted the walls of their caves. Now we have modern paints and brushes and countless painting surfaces to choose from. So why paint a rock?

One of the biggest attractions is being able to pick up great art material that's just lying around free for the taking. Even more exciting is the fact that rocks already have their own unique shapes and sizes. What fun it is to find a rock so perfect for painting that it's almost as if Mother Nature herself had sculpted it for that very purpose.

The projects in this book primarily require rounded rocks, the kind found in creek beds, along rivers, or washed up onto beaches and lake shores. Often hunters and fishermen can tell you where to find these kinds of water-tumbled rocks. If you live in an urban area, your best bet may be to locate a landscaping company or a rock yard that supplies rocks and stones for building projects. They are usually willing to sell individual rocks at low cost and will let you select your own.

Small smooth beach stones sold by the bag offer a variety of shapes and sizes perfect for painting tropical fish. Another option is to collect rocks as you travel. Develop the habit of peering over bridges and paying attention

My rock pile—it's doing double duty as a landscaping element!

to rocks wherever you go. Finding good rocks to paint is a big part of what I enjoy about this art form. It's like a treasure hunt.

Look for rocks that are fairly smooth, without jagged angles or broken edges. They can be as small as a pebble or as big as a boulder, but for most people, rocks that are at least as big as an adult's palm and smaller than a basketball are ideal.

Learning to see how various rock shapes can be used is one of those skills that will improve with practice. Don't be afraid to experiment by sketching designs onto various rocks just to see how they might fit. You can always scrub away your pencil lines and try again. For every project in this book, I offer suggestions as to specific rock sizes and shapes to look for, but

keep in mind that there is no right or wrong way to select or paint on rocks. Feel free to play around with the rocks available in your area to see how you might adapt them to various subjects. You will develop your own individual style of painting your own particular rocks. The instructions I give are designed to help you through the learning process, but they are by no means the only way to achieve attractive results.

SELECTING PAINT

One question that often comes up is, "Can I display my painted rocks outside?" Although the quality of acrylic paints has improved steadily over the years, I always recommended against prolonged exposure to the elements, as it may result in fading or general deterioration. Then I found DecoArt's Patio Paint, a paint formulated specifically to resist weathering and designed for porous surfaces like bird baths, stepping stones and ... rocks! I began using DecoArt's Patio Paint for my own pieces and have been happy with the results. However, there are a few colors not yet available, and for those I've specified other brands. If you don't plan to display your rock art outdoors, there is certainly no reason not to use paints you already have on hand. The conversion chart on this page will help you match Patio Paint colors to those of other brands.

I prefer to work with a limited number of colors, combining them to create variations when needed. An easy way to combine paints into the specified ratios is to cluster paint droplets of the same size on your palette before mixing thoroughly.

SEALER

I am frequently asked how to seal the finished rock artwork. Patio Paint has a brush-on clearcoat, or you may prefer to use clear acrylic in spray-on form. Since my rocks are quite rough, I use a spray-on gloss acrylic from the local hardware store. It enriches the paint colors and provides extra protection. If the rocks in your area are smoother, you may prefer a matte or satin finish to avoid a distracting shine. If you don't paint the bottoms of your rocks (and I usually don't, since I prefer to have naked rock showing), seal the entire rock to prevent moisture from entering. I also recommend resealing your creations once a year if they are displayed outdoors.

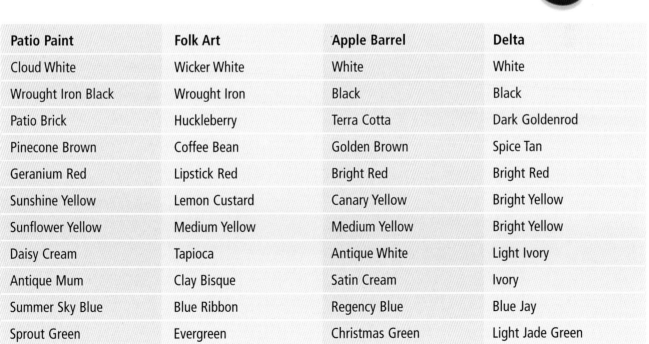

Patio Paint	Folk Art	Apple Barrel	Delta
Cloud White	Wicker White	White	White
Wrought Iron Black	Wrought Iron	Black	Black
Patio Brick	Huckleberry	Terra Cotta	Dark Goldenrod
Pinecone Brown	Coffee Bean	Golden Brown	Spice Tan
Geranium Red	Lipstick Red	Bright Red	Bright Red
Sunshine Yellow	Lemon Custard	Canary Yellow	Bright Yellow
Sunflower Yellow	Medium Yellow	Medium Yellow	Bright Yellow
Daisy Cream	Tapioca	Antique White	Light Ivory
Antique Mum	Clay Bisque	Satin Cream	Ivory
Summer Sky Blue	Blue Ribbon	Regency Blue	Blue Jay
Sprout Green	Evergreen	Christmas Green	Light Jade Green

BRUSHES AND OTHER SUPPLIES

The rocks in my area of the Ozark Mountains are sandstone and have a texture similar to sandpaper. For this reason, I avoid buying expensive brushes. For delicate fur lines and details, my favorite brush is Loew-Cornell's La Corneille Golden Taklon Script Liner Series 7050 in size 0 or 1. The long bristles will hold a lot of paint and I can use the brush on many rocks before the point begins to wear down. Loew-Cornell also makes some stiff, white-bristle craft brushes that are inexpensive and excellent for rock painting. I use wide, flat ones for basecoating and smaller flats for painting in tighter areas. As they wear down or get ragged, I can use them for scrubbing, a drybrush technique used to achieve a soft, diffused look. I've had some success with Silver Brush's Ruby Satin Grass Comb, particularly on smoother stones. Sometimes the bristles on my older brushes will begin to separate from each other, allowing me to make multiple sets of lines with every stroke, a handy time-saver. Other brushes I sometimes find useful include a small round brush for filling in eyes and noses and a larger, soft-bristle brush for applying watery tints.

Recommended Supplies

- Loew-Cornell La Corneille Golden Taklon Script Liner Series 7050, size 0 or 1
- Silver Brush Ruby Satin Grass Comb
- assorted inexpensive stiff, white-bristle craft brushes
- white charcoal or chalk pencil
- regular graphite pencil or black charcoal pencil
- wood filler or putty
- spray acrylic sealer in gloss, semi-gloss, satin and/or matte finish

You will also need white charcoal or white chalk pencils and regular graphite pencils or black charcoal pencils, all for sketching designs. I was given a narrow stick of soapstone that has been great for sketching onto dark rocks or over dark basecoats; these are available through suppliers of welding materials.

Occasionally an otherwise lovely rock is flawed by a hole or crack in an obvious spot. Wood filler or putty, available at most hardware stores, is excellent for filling in such spots and can be painted over when dry. Wood filler can also be used to build up a tippy base. I even used it to add ears to a Yorkie pup rock!

BRUSHSTROKES AND TECHNIQUES

Most pieces use the same simple techniques, all of which can be easily mastered. In watching new painters work, I've noticed a tendency to "sketch" with the brush:

attempting to paint lines via a series of small feathery strokes. If you mix enough water into your paint, you should be able to pull a narrow yet bold line in one single smooth stroke, and in doing so have much better control and smoother, more defined lines.

Practice holding your brush almost perpendicular to the surface you're painting on, allowing the paint to flow off the very tip for crisp, delicate fur lines. Try using your pinkie finger to anchor your hand to the rock as you paint for additional stability and control.

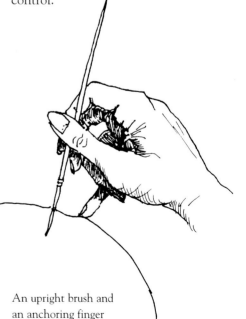

An upright brush and an anchoring finger give control.

PAINT CONSISTENCY

Add varying amounts of water to your paint and practice making test strokes on old newspaper until you can make a dozen or more crisp, narrow fur lines with a single brushload. Once you've gotten a feel for the proper consistency, mixing paint will become second nature.

I paint on top of old newspapers, not just to protect my table, but because it allows me to easily wipe excess paint or water off my brushes and to check the consistency of my paint.

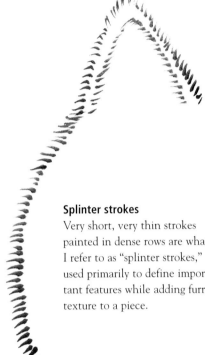

Clusters of fur strokes
To create the look of wavy fur, try clustering sets of strokes that fan out slightly, each set remaining distinct from those around it.

Splinter strokes
Very short, very thin strokes painted in dense rows are what I refer to as "splinter strokes," used primarily to define important features while adding furry texture to a piece.

Layering fur lines
For large areas of fur, create a row of longer strokes, then move halfway up and make another row that overlaps the first. Successive overlapping layers will create the unbroken look of a realistic coat for your animal.

Scrubbed-on paint
Another simple technique, used mainly to create shadows, is to use a stiff or worn-to-a-nub brush with fairly dry paint to "scrub" the pigment into place. Scrubbing with a dry brush yields a soft, diffused look without sharp edges or noticeable brushstrokes.

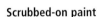

TINTING

Tinting is another helpful technique for softening or altering fur colors. Like hair dye, tinting is a transparent wash loose enough that lighter lines show through while darker colors are unaffected.

As with most skills, practice makes perfect. Experience will give your work polish and added realism. But even new painters can achieve results they'll be proud to show off. Collect photographs of animals. Often by studying a picture I can begin to isolate geometric shapes that will help me to capture the likeness of a particular animal. See the next chapter on painting your pet's portrait for more information on this. Stretch your skills by tackling new subjects and experimenting with various techniques until you find what works best for you. Experience the magic of transforming a rock into a unique piece of art for yourself. I guarantee that you'll never look at rocks the same way again.

pressing down too hard at beginning of stroke

paint too thick or dry

paint too watery or thin

crisp, distinct fur lines

tinted fur lines

Painting Your Pet's Portrait

Perhaps your pet, like our dog Cookie, is a mixed breed. How do you go about determining what shape rock is best for a one-of-a-kind animal? One way is to take photographs of your pet from lots of different angles. As you can see from my photos, Cookie has many expressions and poses. When choosing one of these photos to adapt to a rock, I spread out the photos, selecting those I thought best captured her personality. I always try to figure out how each pose might translate into common rock shapes. Regardless of which pose you choose, a good selection of photographs will make it easier to paint your rock all the way around. I can use the photo in Fig. 6 as a guide for painting the dog's back, for instance, even if I'm painting the pose from Fig. 3.

Fig. 1
One choice is a sitting up pose. However, Cookie has rather large, upright ears, and fitting them onto a rock would require lowering her head, giving her a "hangdog" appearance.

Fig. 2
In this photo, Cookie's ears were down, making for an easier fit. But this is not her most attractive look.

Fig. 3
Here Cookie is crouching with her head turned. By tucking her feet up against her body and wrapping the tail so it curves around her haunches, I can easily see this pose fitting onto a large loaf-shaped rock.

Fig. 4
This photo gives me a view of the head turned the opposite way in case the rock I select is more suited to placing the head on the right side.

Fig. 5
Cookie's head is not turned as far in this picture as it was in the others. This pose doesn't require so many oblique angles, and it might be easier to execute.

SEEING SHAPES

Learning to spot simple geometric shapes in your subject will be a great help in duplicating your pet's features and making your rock look like its model. In looking at Cookie's picture, it's easy to see the triangular shape of her head and the ovals of her muzzle and haunch. Once you've pinpointed these underlying shapes, they can also guide you in keeping the proportions correct because you can compare their sizes to the rest of the animal and get a feel for how they relate to one another.

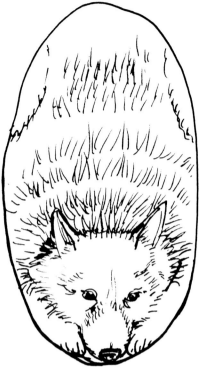

Fig. 6
This photo gave me the idea for yet another pose: Cookie stretched out with her head resting atop her paws. This would work well with a plump, elongated oval rock.

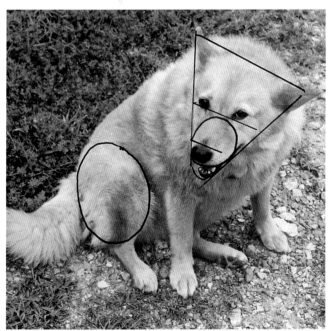

Fig. 7
Superimposing basic geometric shapes onto spare copies of an animal's photo is a great tool for learning how to create your own unique pet portraits. Not only will you be training your eye to recognize those elements as vital building blocks, but they also serve as a guide for achieving proper proportion.

The newest member of our household is Skeeter, a Chihuahua-Pomeranian cross. His portrait could also fit onto a variety of rock shapes. If I were to paint him sitting up, I would darken the area between his front paws, which is the best way to minimize places that you'd like to pretend aren't there. Can you see the geometric shapes in his furry little face?

As with any other endeavor, practice will make a big difference in your results. Give yourself permission to experiment, and keep in mind that it is not possible to ruin a rock! You can resketch and even repaint any rock until you are satisfied with the results.

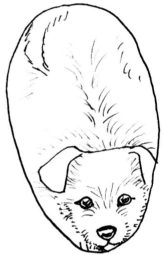

Painting Pets on Rocks

SELECTING COLORS

When it comes to color, new painters are sometimes uncertain and want to be told what colors should be used where. But if your pet isn't one featured in this book, here's a simple technique for determining what colors you'll need to purchase or mix.

Study one of your photographs to determine which color is the lightest. For dogs that are basically one color, the lightest colors will usually be found along the top of the head, back,

and haunches. Cookie's lightest areas (also called highlighted areas) are a very pale cream color that I made by adding a tiny amount of Sunflower Yellow to white paint.

Next, look for the darkest colors. If you find yourself distracted by other details, try cutting a small circle or square from a piece of paper and using it to block out all but the area you want to focus on. Decide what color that area really is. On Cookie, the darkest shadows are a deep brown

with a reddish undertone, so I added black to Patio Brick until I reached a color that looked right. Experiment with mixing colors and dabbing them on clear plastic over your photo until you're satisfied that you've gotten a close match.

Usually the basecoat color will fall somewhere between the darkest and lightest colors. In Cookie's case, the basecoat I selected was a reddish-gold color made by combining Patio Brick and Sunflower Yellow.

lightest color for highlighting

mid-value for basecoat

darkest color for shading and details

In this picture, you can see how these three colors work together to establish the shadows, highlights and contrasts needed to create a realistic fur texture.

Painting Pets on Rocks

How to Paint a
Tropical Fish

Tropical fish are treasured for their jewel-like colors and fanciful designs. It's hard to imagine a color combination Mother Nature hasn't tried. Their wide variety of shapes also make fish an exciting subject for rock painting. Paint individual fish on rocks ranging in size from tiny pebbles to whoppers. Look for rocks that are fairly flat and smooth. River rocks are ideal, but you can transform broken bits of fieldstone into attractive fish art, too. Fish rocks can be as plain or as elaborate as you wish, which makes them ideal subjects for beginning painters and youngsters to tackle!

What You'll Need

- DecoArt Dazzling Metallics in Emperor's Gold
- DecoArt Patio Paint in Wrought Iron Black and Cloud White
- Plaid FolkArt acrylic in Teal
- Plaid Apple Barrel acrylic in Wild Iris
- no. 4 or 6 stiff, flat brush
- no. 2 round brush
- Loew-Cornell script liner, no. 1
- white charcoal pencil
- clear acrylic gloss sealer

1 Choose your rock.
See how I used different sizes and shapes of rocks to represent different types of fish. There are so many kinds of fish, you should have no trouble finding a rock that works. Just make sure it's reasonably flat.

How to Paint a Tropical Fish

2 Lay out your design.

The rock I've chosen is a slightly irregular oval, almost a teardrop shape not much thicker than a fluffy pancake. My rock measures 4" (10cm) long and 3" (7.5cm) wide, about the diameter of an adult's palm. This is an excellent size to begin with as the details will be easy to master.

Use a white charcoal pencil to sketch the fishy features. Since my rock narrows slightly at one end, I'm designating this as the mouth area.

Sketch a circle that begins right at the edge of the rock where the head will be. Leave enough room at the opposite end for a tail fin. The top and bottom fins are formed by the curved wedges remaining above and below the body circle. Keep these fins separate from the tail fin by leaving spaces between them. These spaces, when painted black, will create voids that further define the fin shapes.

Next sketch a half circle to create the head shape. Bisect the end with a slit of a mouth, then add an eye. The size and placement of the eye and mouth can vary from fish to fish.

Finally, add a diamond-shaped side fin just beyond the curve of the head. When you're finished, turn the rock over and sketch a matching design on the other side (or leave it plain).

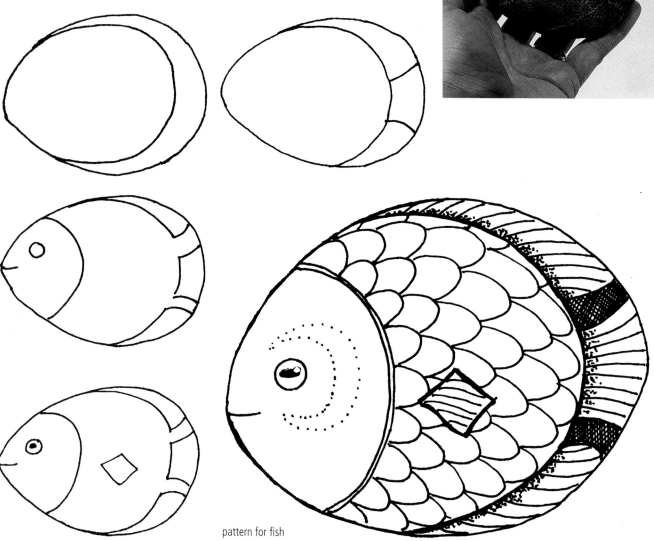

pattern for fish

Painting Pets on Rocks

3 Basecoat the fish.

Use a flat, stiff brush to fill in the body shape with Wild Iris. Make the edges as smoothly rounded as you can. To paint the head and the fins, mix equal parts Teal and white to get a pastel aqua shade. Fill in the head and the fin shapes around the top and the bottom. If you choose to paint only one side of your rock, be sure to wrap the paint around the edges so that no unpainted rock will show. Paint the tail, again wrapping the paint around the end of the rock.

To separate the fins and tail, fill in the spaces above and below the tail with black. Black creates the illusion of empty space.

4 Outline the eye.

Use a script liner and black paint to outline the eye circle. Make the outside of the eye as round as you can. The inside will be covered over.

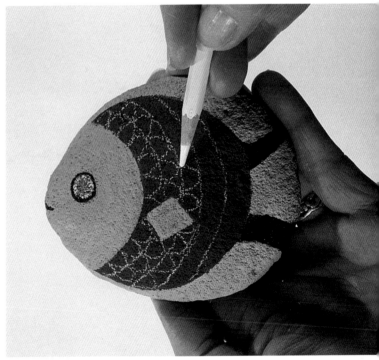

5 Start laying out the scales.

When the paint is dry, use your white charcoal pencil to lightly sketch the guidelines for the scales. Begin by making a parallel curving line just behind the head line. The distance between your lines will dictate the size of your scales. The closer your curving parallel lines, the smaller and more plentiful your scales will have to be. Mine are 1/4" (6mm) apart. Create a series of these curving lines until you reach the tail end.

6 Finish laying out the scales.

Begin with the space between your first line and the edge of the head. Sketch in sideways U-shaped scales. Fit the next row of scales so that each scale begins at the center of the U in front of it and ends in the center of the next one over. Repeat this pattern until the entire body area is filled in. If you aren't happy with your first attempt, simply remove the lines with a damp cloth and redraw them.

7 Paint the scales.

Use metallic gold and your script liner brush to paint in the scale pattern. Add just enough water to your gold paint to ensure that these delicate strokes will flow evenly without breaking or running. Mixing paint to the right consistency is vital for achieving clean, crisp lines. Hold the brush tip nearly perpendicular to the rock surface to keep the strokes from dragging.

You may find it easier to do a two-step stroke, painting half the scale from one side and bringing the other half in from the opposite side. Practicing on newspaper will help you master this stroke.

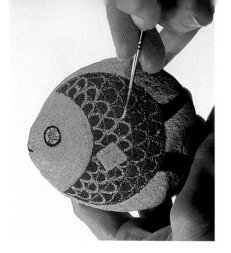

8 Fill in the eye.

While you have gold paint on your brush, fill in the eye circle as well.

9 Define the features.

Switch to black paint, again adding enough water to ensure that your paint flows smoothly. Carefully outline around the body of the fish and around the head circle. Also, outline the side fin.

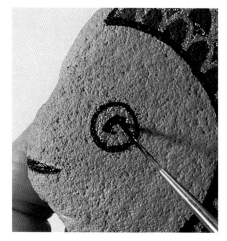

10 Paint the iris.

Give your fish an oval or round iris in the center of the eye. When the iris is exactly centered, you get a more realistic look.

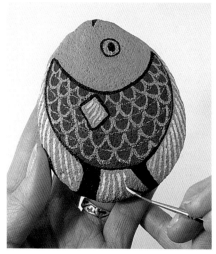

11 Detail the fins.

To detail the fins, create a very pale shade of aqua by mixing a brush tip's worth of Teal into a small puddle of white. Use your script liner to create a series of curving lines angling away from the head toward the tail end along both the top and bottom fins. Fan out narrow lines to detail the tail fin. A set of short, curving lines completes the diamond-shaped side fin.

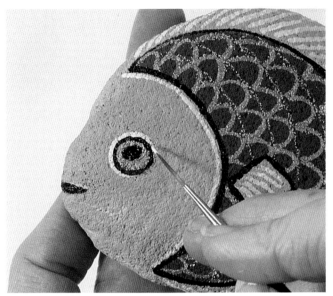

12 Outline the head and eye.

Finally, outline the head shape with this same pale aqua color along the edge of the black outline. Outline around the black eye circle as well.

13 Shade the fin.

Switch to a small round brush to darken the spaces between all the fin lines with straight Teal at their bases. Darken the base of the tail in the same way.

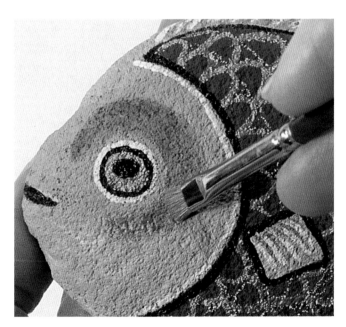

14 Shade around the eye and mouth.

Use your flat brush and more Teal to create a circle of shading that nearly encircles the eye, tapering the stroke at both ends to create a **C** shape that's open facing the mouth. Keep your paint dry for a soft look.

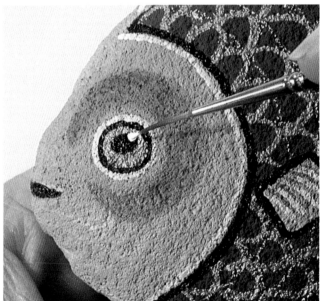

15 Add sparkle to the eye.

Use white paint to dot a sparkle in the fish's eye with the tip of your script liner brush.

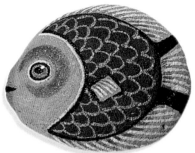

16 Finish the fish.
Remove any remaining chalk lines with a damp cloth before you spray or brush your fish with clear acrylic (gloss, not satin) to give the finished piece a shiny wet look. Sign and date the bottom, or, if you painted both sides, sign your artwork along the edge where the upper or lower fins join.

More Ideas

Squared fieldstones, quarried building blocks, even bricks can all be used to create aquariums filled with colorful fish and green water plants. Paint round or oval river rocks to resemble bowls of fish. Try a strikingly beautiful Siamese fighting fish with a flowing scarf of a tail, or a mini school of neon-bright minnows. I've used glitter paint to simulate sparkling scales on some fish. Tulip's Slick Fabric Paint in the little squeeze bottles added eye-popping three-dimensional details to another. A great project for fish lovers is a goldfish pond created on a large, flat stone. Use DecoArt's Patio Paint to create a deep green background, add contrasting fish and some lily pads, then finish with several coats of protective sealer.

You might even want to try creating an impressive sportman's trophy fish (shown on the opposite page). Mount the finished piece onto an oval board for display. (Drill cement screws through the back of both rock and board to secure your trophy fish.)

No need to change the water in this "fish bowl."

You can turn an ordinary brick into a miniature aquarium.

Glue assorted fish to a painted board. A shadowbox frame and glass will add to the illusion.

The tail fins on this "trophy" fish were cut from a plastic milk jug and attached with wood putty.

Here's my solution for a trouble-free gold-fish pond. Incorporate it into your garden landscape by surrounding it with a border of unpainted rocks.

How to Paint a
Guinea Pig

My first pet was a guinea pig, and many afternoons were spent watching my plump, cinnamon-colored friend graze placidly on our front lawn. Rock guinea pigs make great paperweights or desk art (especially for teachers) or lovable rock pets for youngsters not quite ready to care for the real thing.

Guinea pigs are compact creatures without necks or tails, making them excellent subjects for rock painting. Their simple features and symmetry also make them a good choice for beginning painters. The same techniques for creating lifelike guinea pig fur can be used later on more ambitious animal projects.

What You'll Need

- DecoArt Patio Paint in Cloud White, Wrought Iron Black, Patio Brick, Sunshine Yellow and Geranium Red
- white charcoal pencil
- assorted stiff, flat brushes
- no. 2 or 3 round brush
- Loew-Cornell script liner, no. 1
- spray acrylic sealer

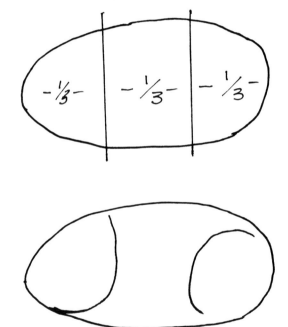

1 Choose your rock.

Begin by looking for rocks shaped like baking potatoes. A slightly tapered or even egg-shaped rock will also work well if it has a flat base. A rock that measures 4" to 8" (10 to 20cm) long is ideal. Working much smaller will result in a pet that risks being mistaken for a hamster or other more diminutive rodent. Examine both ends of your rock and choose the one you think is best suited for the face. If your rock tapers, the slightly smaller end is usually preferred. If both ends are similar, simply use the smoothest and most uniform end.

2 Lay out the design.

Use a white charcoal pencil to lightly sketch the head portion so that it takes up about one-third of the overall length of your rock. If your rock is one of the shorter, rounder ones, the proportions will be more like those of a young piglet whose head takes up not quite half the length. Make the back portion about the same size as the head. The remainder forms the midsection of the animal. Once you've divided the rock as shown, go back and curve the lower portion of the head to create a narrow space beneath the chin where the front feet can be tucked. Round off the tops of the haunches on either side so that they stop about three-fourths of the way up the rock.

3 Draw in the facial features.
Divide the head into quarters vertically and horizontally. Then, divide the two upper sections in half again, creating four pie-shaped wedges. The ears are irregular crescents set at angles so the backs extend slightly beyond the head circle. Rippled edges add realism to the ears. Center them along the lines that divide the top quarters of the head. Keep them fairly small, about as long as the distance between the top points of one wedge.

In the center of the horizontal midline, sketch a shallow, U-shaped nose. Extend a line down from the nose to halfway from the bottom of the rock. Gently curve a mouth line off from either side.

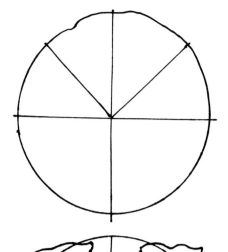

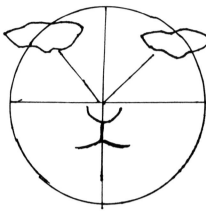

step-by-step layout for head

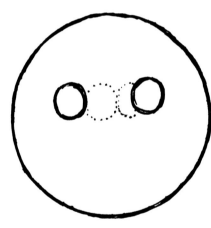

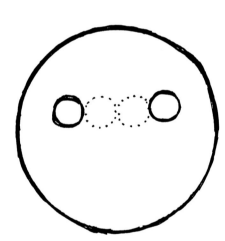

just right

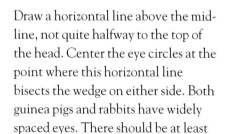

too close together

4 Draw in the feet.
Guinea pigs have well-defined front feet with four small, pointy toes. The back feet are longer than the front ones, and the clustered toes taper to a point. Both sets of feet should be placed along the bottom edges on either side of the rock.

detail of front and back feet

Draw a horizontal line above the midline, not quite halfway to the top of the head. Center the eye circles at the point where this horizontal line bisects the wedge on either side. Both guinea pigs and rabbits have widely spaced eyes. There should be at least two eye widths between them, more if the head end is quite curved. Avoid making the eyes too big. My rock measures $5^{1}/_{2}$" (14cm) long and the eye circles are barely $^{1}/_{2}$" (13mm) in diameter. Oversized eyes will give your pet a cartoon like appearance.

5 Sketch in the fur patches.

Nearly all guinea pigs come in white, a golden or reddish-brown, black or some combination of these basic colors. The variety of patch patterns is endless. You can duplicate my choice or create your own. A white blaze up the middle of the face helps define the features. I chose reddish-brown for one side of the face and part of the opposite side of the back. The other side of the face is black, spreading into a larger patch behind the head, then narrowing to a collar to set off the other side of the head.

6 Paint in the basic color blocks.

Use a stiff, flat brush and white paint to fill in the white patches. Rinse your brush thoroughly, then fill in the black patches. Finally, use Patio Brick, toned down with a small amount of black, to complete the basecoat for the fur. Where the different color patches meet, use the tips of your bristles to lightly feather the borders rather than leaving stark edges.

several views of the color patch layout

How to Paint a Guinea Pig

7 **Paint in the ears.**
To paint in the ears, mix one part Patio Brick with one part white, then add a touch of black to soften the mixture. Switch to a small round brush that allows you to maneuver within the confines of the ears.

ear color

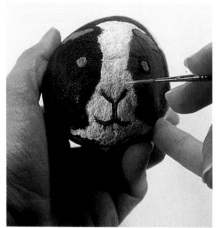

8 **Outline the nose and mouth.**
Paint over the outlines of the nose and mouth, using the same ear color. A script liner brush will make these lines narrow. Be sure to mix enough water into the paint so it flows smoothly.

9 **Paint the nose.**
Mix white and Geranium Red to create a medium pink shade. Stroke upward from the tip of the nose using a slightly dry brush to create a soft transition as the pink fades into the white fur above it.

10 **Paint the feet.**
Use this same shade of pink, slightly thinned, to fill in the front and back feet as well. You may prefer to use a slightly larger brush on the feet for faster application.

11 **Blend the edges of the fur patches.**
To integrate the color patches in a natural-looking way, begin with white paint and a script liner. Start with the white streak between the eyes and make a series of short, delicate fur lines or "splinter strokes." This creates a fringe that angles out and up from the nose. These strokes should vary in length for a random look. As a general rule, animal fur radiates away from the nose, continuing all the way to the tip of the tail. Fur lines that go every which way will create an unkempt look; layers of uniform strokes create a sleek look. Fur lines will be thickest at their beginnings, tapering to a point as the brush is lifted. It may feel more natural to turn the rock as you paint so you're pulling the brush towards yourself.

Painting Pets on Rocks

How to Paint Realistic Fur

The most important elements for realistic fur are the right brush and proper paint consistency. Mix in enough water so the paint flows almost like ink, without being so watery it will run or turn transparent. Practice adding varying amounts of water and making test strokes on newspaper until the paint is thick enough to be opaque yet thin enough to create slender, tapering fur strokes that don't skip or split. When painting, hold your brush nearly perpendicular to the surface of the rock and apply paint from the very tip.

Do the same splinter-type fur strokes with black paint next, so the edges of black patches blend naturally into the neighboring colors. Repeat with more darkened Patio Brick. When you're finished, the edges of all the patches should be fringed with a row of these delicate fur strokes.

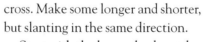

fur direction guide

12 Create layers of fur.
Begin by brightening Patio Brick by adding enough Sunflower Yellow to create a contrasting red-dish-gold shade. It's vital you add enough water to the mixture. Thick paint will clog your brush making strokes look smudgy or fuzzy, not crisp and defined. Strokes may angle toward each other and occasionally cross. Make some longer and shorter, but slanting in the same direction.

Start with the brown back patch behind the head, adding a row of long highlighting strokes along the top and down the sides where the brown and black patches meet. Begin your second row so it partially overlaps the first, and repeat these overlapping layers down the length of the back. These strokes will look best if they vary slightly, so resist the urge to line them up perfectly. Leave a margin around the curve of the haunch unde-tailed for contrast, skipping down to highlight the top half of the haunch itself with rows of fur following the fur direction guide.

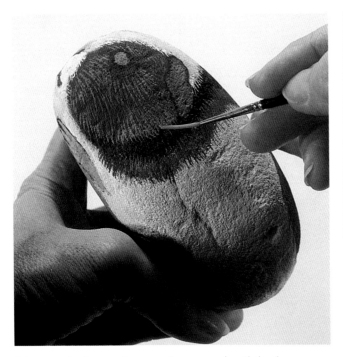

Move to the brown face patch next to detail the features as shown. Be sure to leave a narrow crescent of plain basecoat color below each eye.

To give your brown fur more depth and detail, add enough black to Patio Brick to make a chocolate brown. Use it to emphasize the curved margin between back and haunch, adding several layers of darker fur where the basecoat was left plain. Add another few layers to the lower half of the haunch to suggest shadowing, and to the lower portion of the middle between head and haunch. Also, go over the outlines around all the feet.

Detail the white fur patches using a medium shade of gray made by mixing equal parts of black and white. Gray is used only for shading. Confine your gray fur strokes mainly to the lower portions of the white areas, with a tapered set of dense strokes employed to define the top curve of the haunch.

Use the same shade of gray paint to add furry highlights to the black patch. Leave a dark margin surrounding the eye as before, highlighting just beyond it. Add another curved section of gray fur just beyond the muzzle. Define the head shape with sets of fur lines that begin at the top of the head. Skip over the ear and continue down to end 1/2" (13mm) above the front paw. Keep the outer edges of the black patch undetailed. Encircle the eye with a narrow outline of gray.

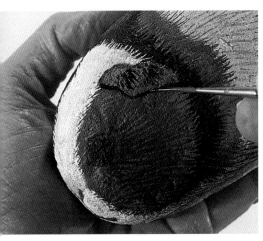

13 Detail the eyes and ears.
Fill in both the eye circles with black paint. Use the tip of your script liner brush and black paint to add a few compact clusters of fur to the ears, then outline around the one on the brown side for added definition.

14 Add the final details.
Switch to white paint and adjust the consistency before making four long whiskers that curve out gently from the muzzle at either side. Soften your white with a touch of black to create a light gray shade, and go around the bottom edges of both ears to set them off. Use the same gray to fan out a set of lines for shading below the chin. Look your animal over to determine if there are any other areas that could use more detailing or defining. The amount and density of the fur strokes is up to you, but the more strokes you make, the more realistic your pet will be.

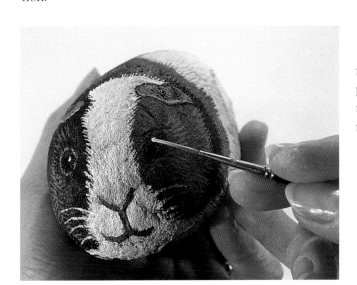

15 Finish the guinea pig.
The last touch is the single dot of white paint near the center of each eye, bringing it to life. When the paint is dry, seal your pet with a coat of clear acrylic. Use matte or satin finish if you are working on smooth, lustrous rocks, gloss if your rocks have texture.

How to Paint a Guinea Pig

How to Paint a Rabbit

Rabbits are similar to guinea pigs and the basic rock shapes are identical. The only differences are that rabbit ears are long ovals placed directly behind the head, and that the feet are blunt oval paws rather than the more rodent-like feet.

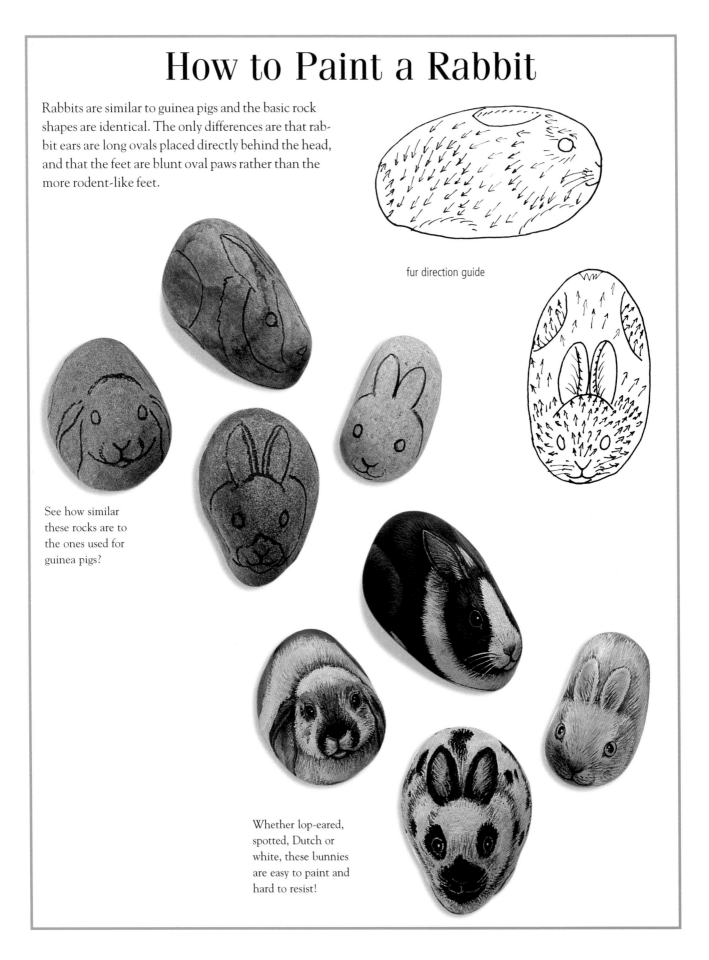

fur direction guide

See how similar these rocks are to the ones used for guinea pigs?

Whether lop-eared, spotted, Dutch or white, these bunnies are easy to paint and hard to resist!

More Ideas

Guinea pigs come in many colors and some varieties have long hair. Domestic rabbits also come in assorted colors and kinds, including lop-eared ones. The hamster is another popular pet that can easily be painted onto a pebble for a "pocket pet."

Wild rabbits are yet another option.

Can't find an oval rock? Try painting twins, or even a whole litter!

Hamster rocks make perfect "pocket pets."

Painting Pets on Rocks

How to Paint a
Parrot

With proper care, real parrots (or macaws) can outlive their owners. Perhaps the same will be true of colorful parrot rocks.

A rock parrot isn't likely to whistle or talk back to you, but he won't need to be fed or have his cage cleaned, either. He won't even need a cage! Instead, let him lend an exotic touch to your decor, or perhaps put him to work as a bookend or doorstop. Displaying parrots in your garden is guaranteed to elicit startled double takes.

What You'll Need

- DecoArt Patio Paint in Geranium Red, Wrought Iron Black, Sunshine Yellow, Summer Sky Blue, Cloud White
- regular graphite pencil
- white charcoal pencil or soapstone
- Loew-Cornell script liner, no. 1
- angular or square chisel brush
- small stiff, flat brushes
- spray acrylic sealer

1 Choose your rock.
When looking for possible parrot rocks, select upright rocks that stand on flat bases. They should taper to a rounded top. If the base flares out to one side, that's a big plus. You may even come across a curving rock that will balance on one of its curves to resemble another birdlike pose.

2 Position the features.

Figuring out how to position parrots on different rock shapes may take some practice. The beak is a prominent feature, so line it up along a corner if your rock has one. With rocks that are more uniform, keep in mind that parrots' heads are ovals that are longer from beak to back. The head can be positioned as though the bird is looking straight out, looking back over its shoulder, or turned as though looking away from itself. Use photographs of actual parrots to help choose the most lifelike pose for your rock.

varying rock shapes

curved rock

I found several potential parrot rocks which stand more or less straight up and one that features a flared base which allows room for tapering tail feathers, making it my choice to demonstrate this project. At the top, my rock has a slightly protruding egg-shaped bulge suggesting the bird could be looking either back over one shoulder or turned sideways to look in the other direction. This second choice allows the frontal display of the colorful wing and tail pattern, making it the more attractive option.

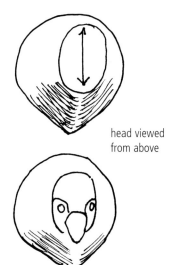

head viewed from above

3 Lay out the head.

The head should take up approximately one-third of the total height of the rock. My rock stands 7" (18cm) tall, so I measured off a head oval that is just under 2" (5cm). Use an ordinary pencil to sketch in the head shape and beak. I've illustrated various head poses. Choose the one best suited to your particular rock. The three-quarter turned head shown at the bottom is probably the easiest and most common.

Copy the appropriate head position onto your rock, being careful to keep the features in proportion relative to the size of the head oval. The beak should take up slightly more than one-third of the total, with the upper curve of the beak extending beyond the head oval. The face patch takes up another third. Since mine is a three-quarter view, a smaller portion of the face patch shows on the other side of the beak; it's a teardrop shape that begins level with the patch on the primary side but remains narrow as it tapers to a point alongside the beak.

possible head layouts

4 Check the features for balance and symmetry.

Draw a straight edge along the top of the beak and set the parrot's eyes into the upper curve of each face patch, resting them on the line formed by the straight edge. This will ensure that the eyes are level and balanced in relation to the beak and to each other. Keep the eyes small to avoid a cartoon look. On my rock the eyes were about the diameter of an ordinary pencil.

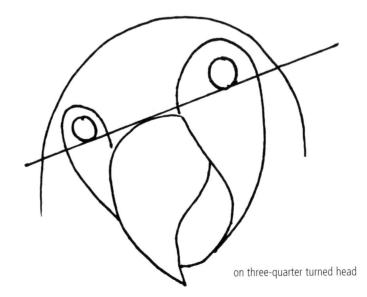

on three-quarter turned head

5 Lay out the body.

Once the head is in place, the remaining features are quite simple. Place the wings just below and to either side of the head, leaving a wide expanse of breast between them. If your rock flares at the base to suggest a tail, the breast should be opposite that tail area. The wing shape is an elongated oval tapering to a slanting point. Square off the tops of the wings. Everything on the backside below the head and between the wings will be the back and tail.

possible body layouts

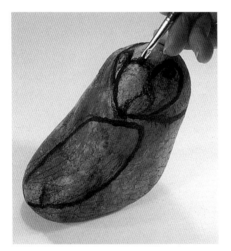

6 Define your sketch.

Once you've completed your layout, go over your sketched lines using the side of a small, stiff, square brush and black paint to make them stand out.

7 Basecoat the parrot.

There are many varieties of parrots and macaws. The one I've chosen is known as the green-wing macaw. Add enough Geranium Red paint to a large puddle of black to get a deep maroon color. Use a large, stiff-bristle brush to fill in every area of your parrot with the exception of the lower two-thirds of each wing, the bottom half of the backside, the beak and the face patches. Don't paint over your black guidelines—leave them for reference and contrast. Paint all the way down to the base of the rock.

8 Begin painting the feathers.

Rinse out your brush and mix small amounts of black into Summer Sky Blue paint until you have a deep navy blue shade. Use this color to fill in the bottom portion of the wings and backside, using your brush to create a ragged border suggesting feathers.

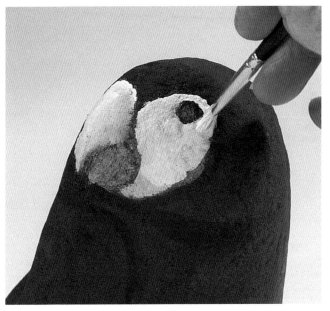

9 Paint the face.

Switch to a smaller brush to fill in the top half of the beak and the face patches with white, leaving the eyes unpainted.

10 Fill in the lower beak.

While the face patches dry, use straight black paint to fill in the lower beak. Also, paint a dark wedge along the bottom of the upper beak corresponding to the lower beak, with the curving top and tip of the beak remaining white. Leave a narrow line of white showing where the two halves of the beak meet to keep each distinct. Check the face patches and add a second coat of white if needed for solid coverage.

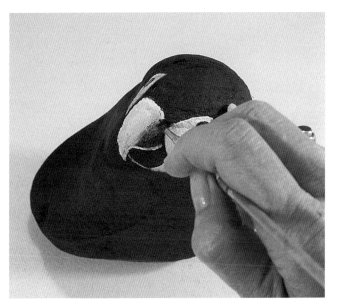

11 Soften the contrast.

Mix a small amount of white into black to get a deep gray and use this color to soften the contrast along the upper beak where the black and white portions meet.

How to Paint a Parrot

detail of feet

12 **Sketch the feet.**
When the basecoat on the breast is dry, use a sharpened white charcoal pencil or soapstone to sketch two elongated, overlapping feet along the very bottom edge of the rock.

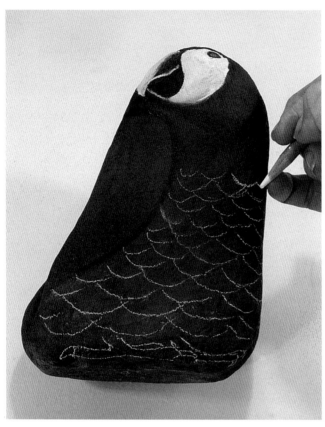

13 **Sketch in feathers.**
Next, create the scalloped look of overlapping feathers on the bird's breast. Begin at the bottom, just above the feet, and make a set of curving lines. Directly above this first set make another row, but start the first curving line so that its midpoint dips down to touch the peak between the scallops below, creating a pattern that continues all the way up to the neck. As you move up, allow the scallops to gradually become smaller and shallower. The scallops do not need to be perfect. Slight irregularities add a more realistic look.

14 **Paint the breast feathers.**
To create a feathered pattern that really stands out, paint an undercoat first. Bright yellow adds warm undertones to the red that follows. Select a brush that will allow you to maneuver in the tight confines of your scalloped pattern. I chose a small square chisel brush that forms a sharp edge when wet. An angular brush will also work well. Use Sunshine Yellow to fill in the scallops, turning your brush as you begin and end each stroke. Note that I did not follow the sketched pattern precisely, merely using it as a guide.

Allow the yellow paint to dry thoroughly. Rinse out your brush and switch to Geranium Red paint to go over the yellow so that no trace remains. Since the undercoat is so dark, don't worry about letting red go beyond the yellow scallops as it will not make much difference. That's why an undercoat is so useful.

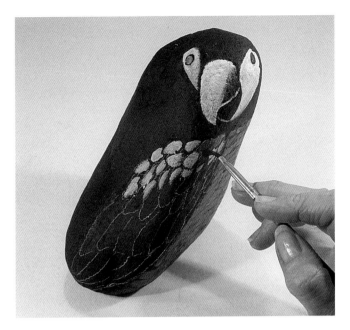

15 Paint the red feathers.

Start sketching at the top of the wings and work your way down. The wing feather pattern is similar to the breast feathers, with the topmost row being the same in both size and scalloped shape. But make the subsequent rows of feathers progressively longer as you work your way downward. Allow a few feathers to overlap their neighbors for a slightly ruffled look, and match up the ends of the final red row to the maroon undercoat. The last two rows of feathers in the dark blue area should be almost bladelike in shape, with the tips of the last set reaching nearly to the base of the rock. Repeat this pattern on the other wing. Once again, undercoat the feathers with yellow, but only those in the areas basecoated with maroon. Leave distinct lines of basecoat between each feather. When dry, go over the yellow areas with red as on the breast.

16 Paint the green and blue feathers.

Undercoat with yellow the first row and half of the second row of feathers in the blue basecoated area. For your next step, rather than overpainting with red, mix a small amount of yellow with enough blue to get a medium blue-green and use this to paint over those feathers. For the blue feathers, add just a touch of white to Summer Sky Blue for more vibrancy. Place a bit more white to one side of this blue and mix up a paler shade. When you fill your brush, add just a little of the lightest blue to the edge of your brush so that when you stroke on each feather, the upper edge will be lighter than the center.

17 Define the feathers.

Mix a small amount of blue with just enough black to resemble the original navy blue base color, and use the very edge of your brush to stroke a line down the center of each blue feather for more definition.

18 Sketch the back feathers.

When both wings are done, move on to the back of your bird. Since my rock flares to one side, the back feather pattern will angle in that direction as it travels downward from the neck. If your rock does not flare out, simply allow the back and tail feathers to proceed straight down. Begin by sketching the looping scallop pattern just below where you've indicated the back of the head ends. After a few rows, begin to allow your back feathers to become longer and more pointed, ending them along the edge of the maroon basecoat.

19 Paint the back feathers.

Paint a bright yellow undercoat for the upper back feathers, again leaving distinct borders between each feather shape.

20 Paint the head feathers.

Use the edge of your square brush or switch to a liner brush to create the look of narrow, almost furlike yellow lines covering the maroon portions of the parrot's head, spacing them closely to fill in the entire area but with minimal overlapping of strokes. The direction of these strokes should move out, down and away from the face patches, slanting sideways as they reach the neck to match the scallops below.

When dry, go over the head with red, but leave the dark undercoat showing around the face patches.

21 Complete the tail feathers.

Return to the back of your parrot to complete the tail feathers. Sketch in several progressively longer and wider feather shapes, perhaps including one at a slightly crooked angle relative to the others. The last row of tail feathers should end at the very edge of the rock. Add horizontal feathers along the base of the rock if needed to avoid having any empty spots. Mix up more of the same blue used on the wing tips, again creating a lighter shade that can be used to highlight the edges of the tail feathers. Mix enough navy blue to add spines to the centers of the tail feathers.

22 Detail the red feathers.

Add detail and texture to your parrot's feathers. Begin by mixing black and red to get a maroon similar to that used for the basecoat. Use the tip of your liner brush to create small fan-shaped clusters of shading along the tops of the scalloped feathers. Remember to add water to your paint to ensure that your strokes remain crisp and delicate. Create the same shading lines below and around each layer of feathers on both upper wings and along the back.

23 Detail the green and blue feathers.
To detail the green feathers, mix yellow and blue to get a bright lime green color. Use this as a highlight, giving each green feather a small spine line and a fringe of highlighting texture along the edges. Leave the areas below and around each feather's base undetailed so that they will seem shadowed by comparison. Similarly, mix up a light shade of blue by adding white, and use it to emphasize the spine lines and to add dense feathery details to the upper edges of each blue feather and sparser details to the lower edges. As with the green feathers, leave the deeper blue undisturbed below and around the base of each feather to suggest shadows.

24 Detail the eyes.
To fill in the eyes, use the same lighter green color used to detail the green wings. Make the eyes as neatly round and symmetrical as you can. Center a black pupil in each eye and add a tiny dot of white to the upper edge of the pupil when it is dry.

25 Paint the feet.
Use white paint to fill in the feet. It may take two coats for solid coverage. When dry, use black paint on the tip of your liner brush to add a mosaic of texture to the feet.

detail of feet

26 **Add the final touches.**
A pattern of delicate red dots surrounding the eyes is a distinctive trait of the green-wing macaw. Make this pattern by using the tip of your liner brush and red paint to first stipple a straight line that begins along the edge of the upper beak then slants down to the lower edge of the face patch. Make two more such lines of dots above the first, each beginning near the beak and following an almost parallel course to the opposite side. At the eye the dotted lines curve to go around on either side, completing the pattern. On the other side of the face, only those dots encircling the eye will show.

Look your bird over from every angle to ensure you have not neglected any areas. When you are satisfied, apply a light coating of sealer to enrich the colors. If you plan to display your parrot outside, be sure to seal the bottom as well.

Many other kinds of pet birds can be painted on rocks—parakeets and love birds come to mind. By using good photographs, the same techniques for handling parrot feathers can be used to create these and other feathered friends. If you're having a hard time finding a good parrot rock, consider painting a double parrot.

More Exotic Animal Ideas

Parrots and their smaller relatives come in a rainbow of gorgeous colors.

Hedgehogs have become popular pets but a painted one is probably easier to cuddle!

A gray basecoat and flesh colored accents helped bring this rock chimp to life.

Box turtles make great subjects. Choose a rock that's dome shaped on top and flat on the bottom.

Like guinea pigs, chinchillas make cute and compact companions.

Ferrets are easiest to paint in tightly curled poses and will be far less mischievous than their live counterparts.

This albino version of a Burmese Python would charm any snake fancier.

See how this rock accommodates my lizard's long tail while the unpainted portions provide an attractive base? Painting in shadows adds to the illusion of dimension.

Painting Pets on Rocks

How to Paint a
Tabby Cat

B old black stripes over a creamy background create an attractive contrast that is both dramatic to look at and exciting to paint. This classic tabby coloring is popular, but the same basic instructions for this project can be used to paint a gray or silver tabby with more subtly shaded markings.

To make this project more accessible to people at varying skill levels, it's presented in three phases. The first requires minimal details and should be easy for even beginning painters to accomplish. People with a little more experience may opt to do the additional fur strokes and details offered in phase two. Experienced painters, or those ready to push on to a new level, can add even more layers of delicate detailing. Regardless of your current painting experience, I hope you'll be inspired to achieve a higher degree of realism with this piece.

What You'll Need

- DecoArt Patio Paint in Antique Mum, Wrought Iron Black, Geranium Red, Sprout Green, Sunshine Yellow, Daisy Cream, Cloud White, Patio Brick, Sunflower Yellow
- 1" and ³/4" stiff, flat brushes
- no. 2 and 4 round brushes
- Loew-Cornell script liner, no. 1
- regular graphite pencil
- spray acrylic sealer

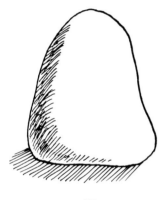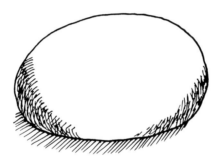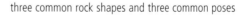

three common rock shapes and three common poses

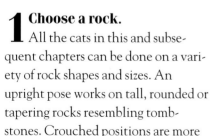

1 Choose a rock.

All the cats in this and subsequent chapters can be done on a variety of rock shapes and sizes. An upright pose works on tall, rounded or tapering rocks resembling tombstones. Crouched positions are more suited to squared, loaf-shaped rocks, and curled cats fit on round or oval rocks. Generally, cats with long hair look best when painted in upright or crouched positions that show their full, furry faces to best advantage. Angular cats, like Siamese and other oriental varieties, often look better in a curled position that allows more room for larger ears. Short-haired cats look great in either curled or crouched poses. It's a little trickier to fit them onto upright rocks, because they lack the fluffy fur coat that helps fill in the wider bottom portions of the rock.

For my cat I've selected an oval rock about 6" (15cm) long, 4" (10cm) wide and 2¹/₂" to 3" (6.5 to 7.5cm) high. Avoid rocks that are less than 2" (5cm) high as your cat will be too flat to look real. Scrub the surface and allow it to dry before applying a basecoat of Antique Mum.

step-by-step layout

layout on round vs. oval rocks

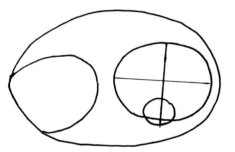

2 Sketch the basic layout.

When the basecoat is dry, use a pencil to sketch in your cat's features. If your round or oval rock is fairly uniform, choose the smoothest side for the head. When one end is higher than the other, I select the high side for the head, since it's the dominant feature.

Begin by making a slightly tilted oval head that takes up a little less than half the front or primary surface of the rock. Tuck this oval right against the outside edge of your rock, allowing plenty of room for the haunch and tail. My cat's head measures 3" (7.5cm) across.

At the other end, sketch in an oval for a haunch, similar in size to the head.

The base of the tail begins just beyond the haunch oval at the bottom edge at the back of the rock. My cat's tail measures about 1" (2.5cm) wide and follows the shape of the rock, curving up slightly as it nears the front edge of the haunch, then curving down and tapering to a rounded end as it nears the center point below the head circle. Fit two elongated oval forepaws so that they tuck into the space below the head.

Note that on a more rounded rock there will be less space between the head circle and the curve of the haunch than on an oval rock.

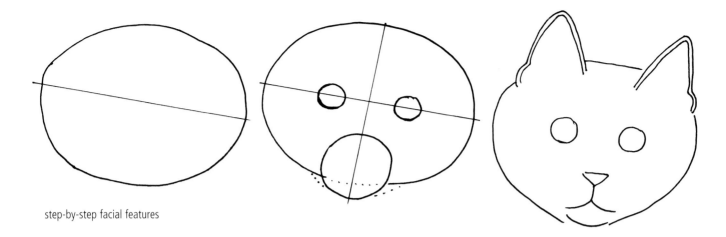

step-by-step facial features

3 Draw in the facial features.

Divide the head oval in half horizontally, angling the line to match the slight tilt of the head. Bisect the oval vertically as well, keeping this line perpendicular to the first so that it's also at a slight angle.

The eyes on my cat measure ¹/₂" (13mm) across. On larger rocks, make the eyes proportionally larger, but keep in mind that overly large eyes will give your cat a cartoonish look. Center each eye over the horizontal line, with at least one full eye width of space between them.

From the eyes, drop down halfway to the bottom of the head, and sketch in a small circle to represent the muzzle. My cat's muzzle is 1" (2.5cm) across, or one-third the width of the head. Allow the bottom portion of this circle to overlap below the head line, forming a small crescent of chin. Fit in a nose triangle so that the top line touches the sides of the muzzle circle near the top, while the bottom of the triangle is even with the vertical line that bisects the head. This will ensure that your nose and eyes are all set at matching angles. Extend a short, straight line from the bottom of the nose triangle, then curve two separate mouth lines off in either direction until they meet the outside edges of the muzzle circle.

The outside edge of each ear should be almost, but not quite, in line with the outermost curve of the head, while the inside line of each ear should line up with the inside edge of the eye below it. On a rock similar in size to mine, the ears should measure 1¹/₄" to 1¹/₂" (3 to 4cm) high.

Before going on, look over your sketched features. Are the eyes the same size and shape? Are the ears symmetrical and properly aligned to the rest of the face? Is the top line of the nose parallel to the line of the eyes? It's a lot easier to make any adjustments now.

4 Create contours.

A ³/₄" or ¹/₂" (2cm or 13mm) flat brush with stiff bristles is ideal for the next step. Surround the head, haunch, tail and paws with a halo of black paint to make these features stand out. Set your loaded brush along the lines you sketched in, pulling away in short strokes, lifting so that the ends are feathered. Once you've outlined all your main features, fill in the space between the chin and haunch with solid black.

5 Paint in the body stripes.

Turn your rock around and begin at the top of the cat's head, stroking in a wide stripe that follows the imaginary spine line as it curves down to the base of the tail. Use the same brush and a series of short, connected strokes to create the cat's stripes. Begin just behind the center of the head and curve the first set of stripe strokes so that a narrow space remains between the stripe and the point of the outside ear. This set of stripes should then run parallel to the side of the face to end level with the outside eye. Curve a matching stripe up and around the inside ear and to end up even with the inside eye. Leave a space the same width as your stripe between each successive set of stripes all the way to the base of the tail. On the tail, make as many stripes of the same width as needed to cover the entire length to the tail's tip.

To stripe the haunch (or haunches if your cat is in a more crouched pose), leave an open space along the rounded top of the haunch, then paint in a series of three to four stripes that tilt downward just slightly.

fur direction guide

6 Paint the face stripes and define the eyes.

On the face, use the side of your brush to pull narrow stripes from the outside edge of each eye to the side of the face. Paint two straight lines from just above the inside corners of the eyes to the top of the head. Add shorter lines that begin just outside those you just made, angling them away slightly. Rough in a few more lines to fill in the remaining area above the eyes. Below the eyes, paint in dark crescents, leaving narrow spaces between them and the eye shapes. Fan a second curving stripe out from the inside end of the first stripe on each side of the face, and a third one that curves the opposite way to outline the muzzle along either side. Switch to a smaller round brush, one that will allow you to neatly but boldly outline the shape of the eyes. Extend a short line down from the inner corners. Also, outline the nose triangle and the curving shape of the mouth.

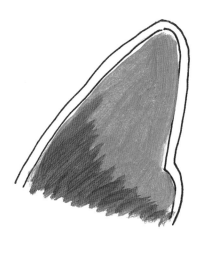

ear color and
shading color

7 Fill in the ears, nose and eyes.

Add a touch of Geranium Red to a small amount of Antique Mum to create a soft pink shade, then add just enough black to tone this pink down. Use a small round or flat brush to fill in the triangular shape of each ear. Create the look of a shadowy base by deepening this dusty pink ear color

with a bit more of both black and red. Use feathery strokes and shade only along the bottom of the ears and up the inside angles to suggest depth. The same color can be used to fill in the nose triangle as well.

Mix Sprout Green and Sunshine Yellow to make a vibrant green and fill in the eye circles, leaving neat black outlines surrounding each eye.

8 Detail the eyes.

Next, darken the green mixture by adding black. Paint a **C**-shaped shadow at the top of both eyes. Clean your brush and mix a much lighter green using mostly yellow. Make a smaller half circle of this highlighting shade along the lower half of each eye. When dry, hang an oval of black from the upper center portion of the eye circle.

9 Add heavy outlines.

Emphasize the eyes by surrounding them with rather heavy outlines of Daisy Cream along both the tops and bottoms, avoiding the dark details. Lighten the top and center of the muzzle along with the chin. Bring out the shapes of the ears by going around them with Antique Mum, but leave a narrow edge of black showing on either side of these lines for contrast.

10 Add muzzle and ear details.

Use a long liner brush or the tip of a stylus to dot curving rows of black follicles across the muzzle. Clean your brush well and add enough water to Cloud White to create a mixture that's loose without being too watery. Test the consistency of your paint on paper first to ensure it flows smoothly without becoming transparent. Pull long graceful strokes from the corner of the base of each ear. Carefully add a set of three to four long, curving whiskers that sprout alongside the follicle dots. Dip the tip of your brush into undiluted white and add one or two white dots to the upper portion of each eye to create a lifelike sparkle. This completes phase one.

Create The Realistic Texture of Fur in Phase Two

11 Add splinter strokes.

Use your long liner brush and loosened Cloud White to begin adding layers of fine fur lines that will give your kitty's coat more texture and contrast. Begin by making what I call "splinter strokes," those short, narrow lines whose bases run together while the tips remain distinct. They help define features the way outlines do, but with a soft, diffused appearance. Make splinter strokes around the top of the haunch and along the top sides of the tail and the paws. Use them to accent the shape of the head all the way around as well. Note that these strokes don't need to be identical in length or thickness, but should be fairly uniform.

To detail the stripes along the cat's body, begin just behind the head and work back towards the tail, using strokes that are longer and more varied than splinter strokes. Allow these strokes to curve and occasionally cross each other in a random and natural-looking way, creating a fringe along the top and bottom edges of the black stripes. Leave the area in the center of the stripes solid black. On the haunch, detail the stripes in the same way.

Shorten the length of your detailing fur strokes back to the size of splinter strokes for the face stripes. Remember that fur always grows out and away from the center of the face, so angle these strokes accordingly as you soften the edges of those markings.

How to Paint a Tabby Cat

12 Detail the black stripes.

Rinse out your brush and begin adding fringes of black fur to the margins of your dark stripes. Allow these strokes to blend and cross the white strokes as they add yet another layer of texture. The tips of these strokes should encroach into the pale stripes of the coat, but keep them sparse so that the contrast between dark and light stripes is not compromised. Don't neglect the tail as you work all the way back up to the head, where you will also want to scatter dark fur details anywhere the white details need softening or blending.

13 Add dimension to the face.

Make the whiskers stand out by adding a narrow outline of black below each one.

Add a new dimension to the face by using a dry round or flat brush and diluted Patio Brick darkened slightly with black to color in the bridge of the nose, sweeping a little color down either side of the nose as well.

This takes your cat to the intermediate level. Once again you can stop here with an attractive piece you can feel proud of, or you can take it to an even higher level of detail.

Finishing Touches in Phase Three

14 Add gold to the body.

Mix Sunflower Yellow into your white paint to get a pale gold color, then add enough water for proper consistency. Use your long liner brush to begin scattering strokes of this warm gold shade into the pale stripes, allowing them to blend with the white fur and the creamy basecoat.

15 **Add gold to the face.**
Add these delicate gold strokes to the light stripes on the face, too. Sprinkle a fan-shaped cluster along the upper bridge of the nose to help blend the reddish-brown areas into the stripes above.

16 **Detail the paws.**
How much the front paws show will depend on your particular rock. Mine are mostly hidden but I felt they needed more work, so I added several overlapping layers of golden fur lines to each paw, then used black to add a couple of rather sparse dark stripes.

17 **Add the final touches.**
Soften your black with enough Patio Brick to create a deep brown, and stroke in a set of very delicate splinter strokes where the mouth lines meet the chin to suggest gentle shadowing there. I also added a few fanned out lines to the center of the nose.

Look your cat over from every angle to ensure that you've added sufficient furry details. A light spray of clear acrylic sealer will add luster and enrich your colors.

Painting Pets on Rocks

How to Paint a
Black Cat

Painting any solid black animal presents a perplexing problem. How do you indicate various contours and shapes without turning black into gray? For this black cat the solution is to create the look of subtle sheens simulating the play of light over the features. Add a pair of startling amber eyes and the effect is riveting.

What You'll Need

- DecoArt Patio Paint in Wrought Iron Black, Cloud White, Summer Sky Blue, Sunflower Yellow, Sunshine Yellow and Geranium Red
- assorted stiff, flat brushes
- old ragged brushes (or a ¼" Silver Brush Ruby Satin Grass Comb)
- no. 4 round or flat brush
- Loew-Cornell script liner, no. 1
- white charcoal pencil
- spray acrylic sealer

1 Choose a rock and basecoat it.

Black cats can be painted in either curled or crouched positions. A crouched pose looks best when displayed up off the floor, while a curled pose is most effective when viewed from above. Look for rocks that have some height to them, similar to a loaf shape. One end may slope down, but at least one end should have enough height to allow room for a head, ears and all. The rock I chose is loaf-shaped, nearly 8" (20cm) long, 3" (7.5cm) wide and 5" (12.5cm) tall. Practice sketches help show how your cat might fit. Scrub your rock and let it dry. Use a large damp brush to completely cover the entire visible portion of the rock with solid Wrought Iron Black. Completely fill in any pits or irregularities as unpainted places will really show up under strong light.

2 Lay out your design.

Look your rock over, selecting the smoothest site for the face. The head should take up a little more than a third but less than half of the total frontal surface visible (for more rounded rocks the front surface will also include the curving top). Use a white charcoal pencil to make a plump oval head that sits far enough down to leave room for the ears. If your rock is quite flat across the top, it's especially important that there be room for the ears. Otherwise, your cat is liable to look earless when viewed from certain angles.

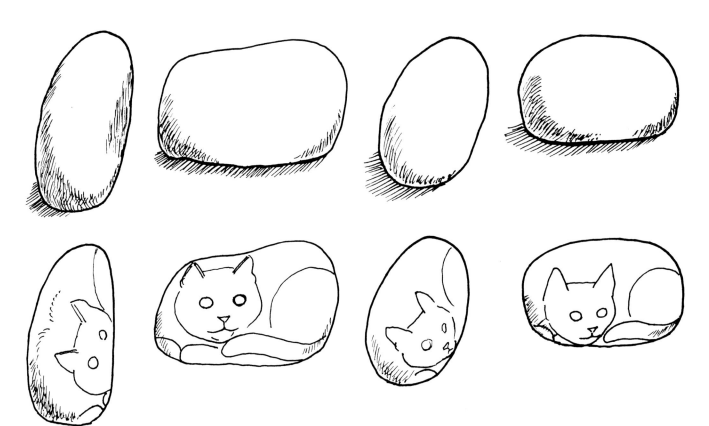

possible layouts for various rock shapes

Painting Pets on Rocks

Bisect the head oval horizontally and center two round eyes on that line. Leave one and a half eye widths between the two eyes. From the inside corner of each eye, run an imaginary line straight up to the top of the oval, and start the inside edge of each ear from that point. Extend the ear lines down into the head oval by $1/2$" (13mm) or so to keep them from looking precariously perched there. On my cat, the ear triangles measure $1^1/2$" (4cm) from base to tip, and are nearly 1" (2.5cm) wide at the bottom, with the outside edge of the ear attached to the head oval about halfway between the bisecting eye line and the top of the head. Drop down from the eye line to center a small nose triangle so that the bottom is even with the midpoint between the eye line and the bottom of the head oval. From the nose make a short, straight line that drops down, then splits in two, each side curving back to form the muzzle just before reaching the bottom of the head oval.

Sketch a slightly more flattened oval along the opposite end of the rock to indicate the haunch, and bring a thick, sturdy tail up from the base at the end of the rock, curving it slightly before ending it just below and to the side of the head. Indicate a rear foot like an elongated oval beneath the tail. For front paws, add two more ovals, slightly wider than the tail, tucking them in the remaining area beyond the tail tip.

On the backside of the rock, make a matching haunch and rear foot.

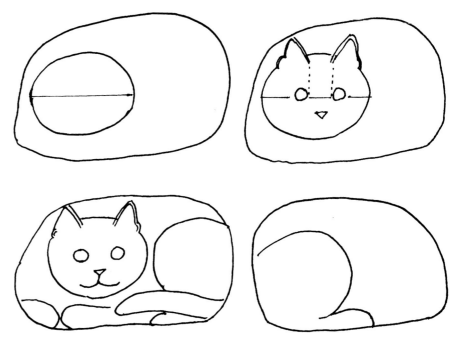

step-by-step layout

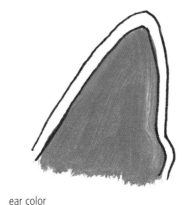

ear color

3 Fill in the ears.
Use a small flat brush with stiff bristles to mix a tiny amount of Geranium Red into a scant puddle of white paint for a medium shade of pink. A trace amount of black will tone this pink down to a dusky shade. Use this color to fill in the ear triangles. Don't paint out to the edges—leave an outline of black around each ear.

How to Paint a Black Cat

 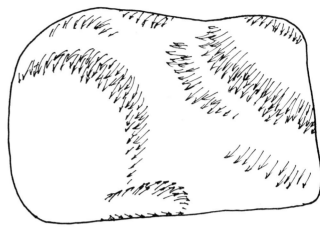

4 Create the illusion of contours.

Select your most ragged stiff, flat brush or a grass comb and mix a very deep shade of gray. Experiment on newspaper to find the mixture of paint and water that gives the look of sets of individual lines with every stroke. Starting with the back side of your cat, create a wide, unbroken swath of these short, highlighting stokes following the curve of the haunch. Consult the fur direction guide to ensure that these strokes angle in the natural way fur would lie. Curving your strokes slightly will give the haunch added dimension.

Leave the lower half of the haunch dark, but add a sheen to the top of the rear foot. Still on the backside, move up to add a set of wide, curving highlights along the top and a curving diagonal swath almost parallel to the haunch, again checking the fur direction guide so that your strokes correspond to the way fur grows in these areas.

Now turn your rock around to the front and define the head by adding a soft sheen at the top and down both sides. Add volume by making a curving series of sheen strokes around the top of the haunch, as well as along the tops of the tail and the front paws. Leave a dark margin all the way around the outside of the head and ears as you lightly stroke in the sheen of shoulders behind them. Note that these strokes should angle upward and outward as indicated in the fur direction guide. At the cat's tail end there may be room between the two haunches for another, more abbreviated, sheen, but remember to leave dark spaces in place between them for contrast.

5 Detail the head.

Add enough white to the gray you've been using to lighten it noticeably. Switch to a script liner brush and add enough water to your paint to achieve a consistency that flows readily from the tip of your brush, yet is not so watery that it runs or becomes transparent as it dries. Begin along the edges of the ears, making delicate splinter strokes so closely spaced that they blend into one another in a continuous prickly line, creating the look of velvety texture while defining the ears. Leave a narrow outline of black showing between the outline and the pink ear color. Along the outside edge of each ear, stop just short of the head and add a small scallop that curves out from the ear line then drops to complete the ear. Outline the nose triangle and cluster a few longer lines above it in an inverted fan shape to indicate the bridge of the nose, ending the lines about level with the line of the eyes. Next, go to the chin area and use a tiny, cupped line to indicate the gleam of a bottom lip just below where the muzzle lines divide. Fill in the chin area with a series of tiny strokes that fan out from just beyond a narrow dark space left to define the lower lip. Layer on more several tight rows of fanned-out strokes until the chin area is clearly defined with fur. Below each eye circle stroke a narrow rim of gray. From the inside corners make a short stroke, almost like a dash, or tiny triangle, pointing down toward the nose.

6 Add more splinter strokes.

Work around the shape of the head with delicate splinter strokes but make them less dense, radiating out like short sunrays. A second, even sparser layer half-overlapping the first (from the inside) should define the head between traces of the underlying highlighting sheen.

7 Define the facial contours.

Use your script liner brush to create subtle highlights, giving the face an indication of underlying bone structure. A row of slanting strokes beneath each eye highlights cheekbones. Give the muzzle contour by highlighting the edges with splinter strokes. Also, highlight the center of the muzzle, leaving dark edges around the nose triangle and between the two halves of the muzzle. Create several layers of highlighted fur in the space directly below the outside ear. Extend the lowest set of these strokes down into the area between the eyes and then back up above the other eye. Leave an undetailed dark place at mid-forehead to provide contrast.

8 Detail and define the cat's coat.

Add texture and emphasis to the sheen areas on the cat's coat by using your script liner brush and the same light gray paint to add fur lines, beginning along the shoulder blades. Create several layers of longer, but still delicate, fur lines along the outer edges of the sheen areas. Bring a delicate set of fur strokes down into the space between head and haunch to keep it from seeming bottomless. Leave the dark margins undefined, skipping over them to work your way toward the tail as you highlight the leading edge of each subsequent sheen area. Along the curve of the haunch concentrate your fur lines to help accentuate this important element.

Add longer highlighting fur lines along the top of the tail if needed to set it off. Then, go back to the base of the tail and create a dense line of shorter, splinter strokes that define the bottom edge of the tail. Use the same technique to detail the front and rear paws, and add a necklace of fur lines in the area showing between the head and the front paws, extending these lines as you curve them around the rock where the cat's chest would be. Don't neglect the backside of your rock, again highlighting the outside edges of your sheen areas, including those along the haunch and rear foot.

It may be difficult to paint these strokes and still achieve a smooth edge along the top of the haunch. If so, simply go back later with black paint and run a line along the outside edge to smooth it down.

9 Tint the gray highlights.

To keep these gray highlights from turning your black cat into a gray one, you can use a simple method that tones them down without losing the texture they provide. Use a large flat brush to mix up a watery tint consisting mainly of Summer Sky Blue with just enough black to create a deep blue-black. Your tint should be so transparent that a test stroke on newsprint allows the letters to show through clearly. It may require some experimentation to find just the right mixture of pigment and water. If your tint is too blue, simply blot it up quickly, add water and a bit more black paint, then try again. Use this blue tint to blend and soften any areas of the coat and face that may have gotten too light, but avoid tinting the fur lines at the outside edges of your features.

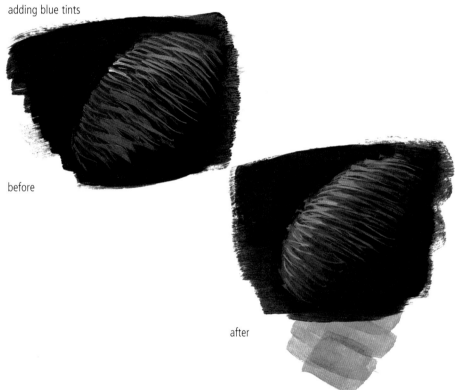

adding blue tints

before

after

10 Retouch with black.

Look your cat over for places where your highlighting strokes may have intruded into the dark spaces, lessening the needed contrast. Usually a few dark strokes are enough to correct this. Scatter a few dark fur lines among the lighter ones along the forehead, around the eyes and in the shadows surrounding the head. Add some dark fur lines down the center of the tail and along the paws, so their dark tips blend into the highlighted fur. Try adding some to the centers of each muzzle area, too. You may also need to redefine the tail where it overlaps the front paw to ensure that these two elements are clearly separate.

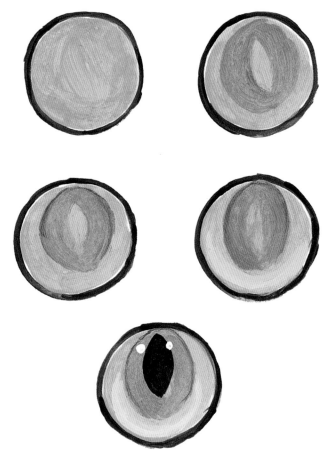

12 Add ear whiskers.
While you have black paint on your brush, add a cluster of dark ear whiskers to the bottom and inside edges of the ears, fanning the whiskers out from the corners.

11 Paint the eyes.
Black cats can have green or orange eyes, but my favorite choice is a bright amber with orange shadows. They practically glow in the dark!

Use a small round brush to fill in both eyes with Sunflower Yellow, leaving a narrow outline of black showing in between the eye color and the gray underlining. It will probably take two coats to get solid coverage. Allow the first to dry before applying the second. Next, add just enough red paint to Sunshine Yellow to make a nice bright shade of orange. Make an inner half circle of orange that just touches the top of the eye, leaving a wider edge of yellow showing in the bottom portion of the eye. With the tip of your script liner brush, add a trace of red to the orange you mixed and use this darker red-orange to outline around the top of the orange half circle. Rinse out your brush and mix a bit of straight Sunshine Yellow with a smaller amount of white to create a bright pale yellow. Use this to create a highlighting ring along the very bottom of each eye, just beyond the orange ring. When the eyes are dry, add a small, oval black pupil to each eye, placed so the top almost brushes the top of the eye, making the cat appear to be looking up.

13 Add the whiskers.
Adjust the consistency of the white paint until it flows smoothly, then apply three or four long narrow whiskers, beginning within the darker area of the muzzle and arching them slightly as you stroke outward beyond the edges of the head. If your whisker lines get too thick, underlining with black will allow you to shave down any excess white.

14 Add the finishing touches.

Check to make sure that there is still a very narrow edge of black showing around the bottom of each eye between the gray rims and the actual eye color. It should be smooth and unbroken all the way around, so go over it if needed. Switch to white paint and dab one or two dots on either side of the upper pupil in each eye. Now look your cat over, paying attention to both ends and back to ensure that you have created enough fur details for a realistic look from every angle. Black cats really benefit from the application of a coat of sealer that will deepen the dark shades further and add gloss to the coat. If you're painting on smooth rocks, use a matte or satin finish rather than gloss to avoid creating glare. Seal the bottom as well if you plan to display your cat outdoors.

How to Paint a White Cat

Elegant white cats have come to symbolize the most indulged and pampered of pets. Something in their calm gaze seems to assert, "I may be high maintenance, but aren't I worth it?" Long fluffy fur makes this cat a perfect candidate for painting in a sitting pose.

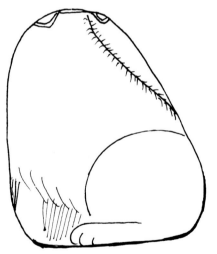

Look for upright rocks that have one flat end to serve as a base and enough height to fit a head at the top, with room for a haunch, feathery chest and two short front legs below. It could almost be a tomb-stone shape, although symmetry is not necessary or even preferred for this project. The rock I chose slopes along one side while the opposite side is more vertical. Overall, my rock measures 5" (12.5cm) high, 3" (7.5cm) thick and is a little over 5" (12.5cm) wide at the broadest point.

1 The features of black animals are defined by subtle sheens while solid white animals depend instead upon the use of delicate shading. Begin by mixing black and white paint to get a medium gray color, then warm it up by adding a brushful of Pinecone Brown. Cover the entire rock with a basecoat of this color. Sketch on your design, and create added dimension by using a darker shade of gray to suggest more depth as shown. Stroke outward from these features to create feathered edges.

2 Next use a stiff or scruffy brush and white paint to highlight those areas that would be the most purely white. Again, pull your strokes outward, allowing the edges to feather.

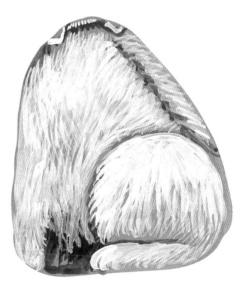

3 Switch to a script-liner to augment the feather edges with additional, longer fur lines, extending them into the solid gray areas to create a blended effect. Leave more gray showing through along the lower portions to suggest shadowing. By alternating sets of gray and white fur lines, you can first define the muzzle area and the shadows around the eyes, then soften and blend them until a balance is reached where the cat's features are discernible, yet the overall effect is so softly understated and the highlights so pure that there is no mistaking it for a gray cat.

4 On the backside use white paint on your stiff brush to create two sets of lines flowing out from either side of a gray spine line.

How to Paint a Black Cat

Painting Pets on Rocks

How to Paint a
Siamese Cat

Purebred Siamese cats are lean, graceful creatures with softly shaded coats and distinctive features that put them in a class by themselves. These cats often have long, whip-like tails, angular heads, tilted eyes, large ears and straight, prominent noses. Siamese come in a variety of hues, the names of which refer to their points, meaning the head, feet and tail areas. As with other short-haired cats, Siamese look best in curled or crouched positions. A curled pose is my first choice because it allows plenty of room for those imposing ears. The greatest challenge in painting Siamese cats is duplicating the subtle blending and shading of their coat colors.

What You'll Need

- DecoArt Patio Paint in Antique Mum, Geranium Red, Woodland Brown, Wrought Iron Black, Daisy Cream, Summer Sky Blue, Sunflower Yellow, Cloud White, Light Waterfall Blue (optional)
- assorted large and medium stiff, flat brushes
- no. 2 or 3 small round brush
- Loew-Cornell script liner, no. 1
- graphite pencil
- white charcoal pencil (optional)
- spray acrylic sealer

1 Choose a rock.

For Siamese cats, choose a round or oval rock that is on the thin side, perhaps with some rounded angles suggestive of the sleek athletic build of a healthy, active feline. You can work as large or as small as you wish, but for this demonstration I chose an oval that measures 5" (12.5cm) long, 4" (10cm) across and is just a little more than 2" (5cm) high. Scrub the rock and let it dry. If you are uncertain about where to place the head, try using a white charcoal pencil to experiment with possible combinations. Knowing that you'll be painting over your sketch may help you loosen up as you decide how best to use your rock's unique contours.

2 Paint the basecoat.

Use Antique Mum and a large flat brush to cover the entire upper surface of the rock, leaving only the very bottom unpainted. (For a blue- or lilac-point Siamese, try mixing Cloud White with enough Light Waterfall Blue to get a very pale blue-gray shade for the base.) Allow the basecoat to dry.

3 Sketch the layout.

Envision a broad triangle and you have the basic wedge shape of a Siamese cat's head. For my cat the sides of the head each measure 3" (7.5 cm). Set the head low enough to leave ample room above for the ears. Begin the bases of the ears below the top line of the head so that they appear to be integral rather than perching on top. My ears are 1¹⁄₄" (3cm) high measured from the middle, and nearly that wide at the base. Rest the eyes atop a horizontal line midway down the triangle. On my cat the eyes are ¹⁄₂" (13mm) long. Leave slightly more than one eye width between the eyes. Pull a horizontal line out from the top outer edge of each eye, and extend a slanting line from the inner corners to give the eyes their almond cast. The bridge of the nose begins with a narrow pair of lines at eye level. Slightly flare the lines out as they go down, creating a nose about as long as the space between the eyes. Set a small triangular nose leather at the end. There should be just enough room at the bottom angle of the head to fit two curving mouth lines that define the muzzle. Remove the point at the bottom of the head triangle, turning the end into a half round chin. Add curves to soften the sides of the face on either side.

Sketch an oval haunch into the space next to the head. The more elongated the rock, the larger the space will be between head and haunch. A thin, ropey tail is characteristic of many pedigreed Siamese. Bring it in from near the base below the edge of the haunch, curving it gently as you angle it up toward the side of the face, then hooking the tip back in a **J** shape. Tuck two long oval paws beneath the head.

Before going on, place a pencil even with the eyes and another level with the top of the nose. The pencils should be parallel to prevent an off kilter or skewed look. If not, it's easiest to simply change the angle of the nose.

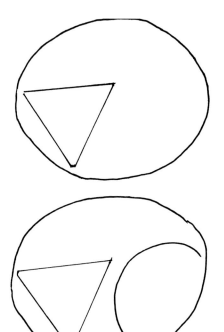

step-by-step layout

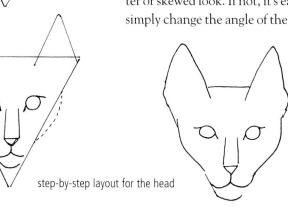

step-by-step layout for the head

Painting Pets on Rocks

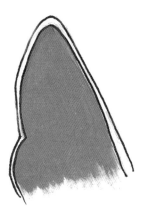

4 Paint the insides of the ears.

Mix a small amount of Geranium Red into a larger puddle of Antique Mum to create a soft pink. Darken this pink shade by adding small increments of Woodland Brown until the color resembles a ruddy flesh tone. Use a round or flat brush to fill in the entire triangle shape of the ears, allowing your brushstrokes along the bottom to be slightly ragged.

5 Paint the points.

Use Woodland Brown and a stiff, flat brush to create a solid mask around the eyes. Darken the muzzle areas and the chin, joining them to the brown mask above. Extend a short, thick line from the top of the eye mask to touch the inside corners of both ears. Paint both front paws and the tail dark brown.

6 Create contours.

Pick up more brown paint, using the same stiff, flat brush. Remove any excess by wiping on newsprint to keep the paint on the dry side. Scrub this paint out from around the head and haunch so that those features are surrounded by a slightly diffused dark halo. Darken the area between the bottom of the head and the curve of the tail, leaving only the narrow wedge between tail and rear foot unshaded.

Turn your rock around and scrub in a curving spine line beginning behind the head and following the natural contour of the rock to the base of the tail. Add two wide, rounded U shapes to represent the shoulders of the cat, and if there's room, skip a space then add a second shaded line, less curved this time, closer to the tail.

Finally, remove even more paint from your brush by wiping it vigorously on newspaper before you scrub soft, diffused brown along the top half of the haunch. Make the strokes at the bottom uneven, blending them into the lighter basecoat.

7 Define the face.

Switch to a long script liner and black paint. Add enough water to ensure the paint flows easily without becoming transparent or runny. Outline the eyes, emphasizing those accenting lines extending from the corners. Go around the top angles of the ears to accent them, adding an extra scallop to the outside edges near the base. Define the long bridge of the nose, then fill in the nose leather at the end. Outline the mouth lines.

8 Emphasize with fur lines.

Rather than using solid outlines, define the paws and tail with the texture of fur. Paint in dense sets of short, splinter type strokes that follow the natural direction of the fur (refer to the fur direction guide).

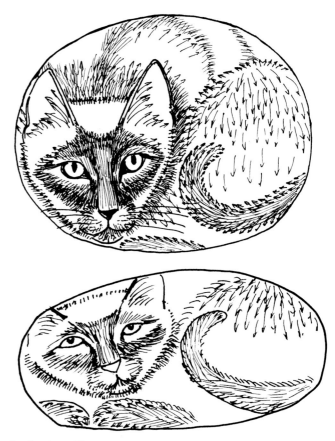

fur direction guide

Painting Pets on Rocks

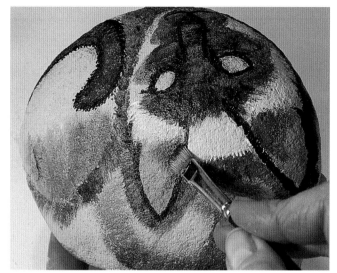

9 Shade inside the ears.

To give the ears depth, use a stiff brush and a combination of brown darkened with black, blotted almost dry. Smudge this color along the base of the ears, fanning up and out from the inside corners. Since these are shadows, they should look soft and blend gradually into the rest of the ear.

10 Create fur texture on the head.

Daisy Cream is a warm, off-white shade that offers a subtle yet effective contrast to the Antique Mum basecoat. Adjust the texture of the paint by adding water and mixing thoroughly until the consistency is loose without being runny. Use the tip of your script liner brush to apply fur lines that are narrow, but not quite as short or dense as splinter strokes. Apply them in overlapping layers like thatch, working your way from the outside edges inward to cover the face around the mask. Again, you may find it helpful to turn the cat around so that you can stroke toward rather than away from yourself. Consult the fur direction guide to help simulate realistic fur growth patterns. Allow some fur lines to touch or cross, but leave spaces between the strokes so that the basecoat shows through. When you reach the face mask, the tips of the fur should slightly overlap the edges of those dark areas.

11 Create fur texture on the body.

On the haunch, begin by outlining the outside curve with the same strokes used around the head, making them a bit longer. Move to the bottom of the haunch and stroke layer upon overlapping layer of cream-colored fur lines. Pull these strokes out toward the edge of the haunch so the fur tapers at the tips. As you reach the upper, darkened portion of the haunch, your fur strokes should create a seamless blending of lighter and darker areas. Allow fur lines to become gradually sparser until, at the top, you sprinkle in a few for continuity, leaving most of the dark undercoat exposed.

too much initial pressure can create knobs on your fur strokes

12 Detail the back.

This fur will be much easier to paint if the rock is turned around. Begin your first fur lines just inside the dark shadows surrounding the head. Use the fur direction guide to aid in determining how to angle the strokes as you apply layer upon layer until the tips of your strokes reach into the next area of contouring brown at the shoulders. Skip down to the next area of basecoat and repeat the process until the entire back portion of the cat has been detailed.

13 Detail the remaining areas.

Move to the area between the curving tail and lower portion of the face. Leave a margin of brown contouring shadows untouched, using narrow overlapping fur lines to soften the contrast between dark and light areas. These strokes should follow the curving shape of the rock, becoming more sparse near the area between paw and tail.

Turn to the other side of the head and again soften the dark shadows by adding a fringe of pale strokes along the edge. Continue to add more fur layers until you reach the bottom edge of the rock.

14 Add more definition to the face.

Add enough black to Woodland Brown to get a deeper dark brown. With a script liner brush, add several delicate layers of fur lines around the inside edges of the mask and muzzle, with just the tips extending beyond the mask. Add long, dark fur to the inside corners of the ears, then make shorter fur up both inside edges. Move out to the shadows around the head itself and add dark fur texture to the brown shading all the way around.

15 Continue detailing.

Lightly scatter some dark fur lines around the top of the haunch, with just a few more sprinkled about the middle portion. Several overlapping layers along the lower half of the tail for shadowing will suggest volume. Do the same along the lower half of the paws.

16 Add white fur details.

Loosen a small amount of Cloud White paint with enough water to achieve the right consistency for crisp strokes. Fan out long, delicately curving ear whiskers from the inside corners of each ear, overlapping the darker lines you made previously. Add a row of white fur below the base of the ear as well. The judicious and sparing use of white can heighten contrast in other areas, too. These areas include the edges of the head, the top curve of the haunch, the tips of the shoulders and along the edges of any other contrasting dark areas along the back. Trust your eyes to direct you to areas that would benefit from more emphasis. Several loose layers of white fur in the lower half of the haunch will brighten that area.

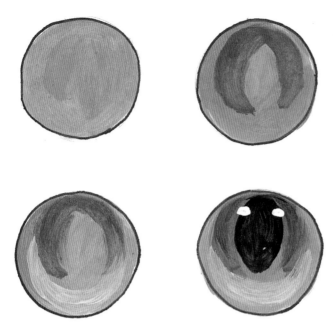

18 Accent the nose and eyes.
To warm up the face area and bring out the eyes, lighten a small amount of Woodland Brown with enough Sunflower Yellow to create a golden brown color. Apply this color with a round or flat brush, first to the bridge of the nose to pull it out from the face, then above and below each eye.

17 Paint the distinctive Siamese eyes.
Vivid blue eyes are as much the hallmark of the Siamese cat as its shaded coat and contrasting points. Select a brush suitable for filling in small, tight areas, such as a round brush in size 2 or 3. Pour out a small amount of Summer Sky Blue and matching amount of Cloud White. In a separate area, mix a brushful of each color together to get a medium blue. Fill in the almond shapes of the eyes, being careful to leave a defining outline of black surrounding them. The edges of the eyes should be as smooth and uniform as possible. If needed, you can go back after they are dry and neaten up by reapplying the black outline. Rinse your brush and take up a small amount of Summer Sky Blue. Add just enough black to get a color somewhere between royal and navy blue. Don't make it too dark or the black pupil will not show up against it. Use this to create a second, smaller half circle that extends from the top of the eye. Again rinse, then blend more white with a touch of blue to create noticeably paler shade. Form a half circle of this light blue in the lower half of the eye, leaving a narrow edge of the original blue eye color showing around the edges. When dry, add a small oval of black that hangs suspended from the top of the eye and just overlaps the highlighting half circle below. Many Siamese have crossed eyes, and should you want to paint this trait on your cat, simply move each pupil slightly off center towards the nose.

19 Accent the body.
Blot your brush and scrub this lighter brown lightly along the top portion of the haunch, avoiding the outside edges. Also, scrub behind the head and along the top edge of the face mask to create a diffused look. Add a bit of this tint into the area just below where tail and cheek meet, and any other place where it seems the fur lines could use a bit of subtle blending.

20 Add fur lines.
With a script liner, add golden brown fur lines to the top edges of the paws and tail.

21 Add whiskers.
Rinse out your brush and add one or two dots of white to the upper center of each eye. Loosen your white paint with water until the consistency is right for creating a set of long, elegant whiskers flowing out from within the muzzle area. If your whiskers get too thick, try shaving them down with an underline of dark brown. I also added a bit more dark fur to my cat's cheekbones in order to blend the edges of the highlighting there.

22 Complete a final check.
Look your cat over from every angle, searching for any areas that seem to need more detailing or defining. When you are satisfied, sign your piece and give it a sealing coat of clear acrylic to protect and enhance the colors.

Create an entire Siamese family.

More Cat Ideas

Placing two or more cats on a single rock makes for an arresting piece.

A cat sleeping on its back is another appealing pose you might want to try.

Once you've mastered the basics, you can paint any kind of cat or kitten. The cat on the far left features a second oval rock for a tail.

Cat Portraits

Here are a few recent cat portraits along with the photos I used to paint them.

How to Paint a
Dalmatian

With their dropped ears, boxy foreheads and blunt muzzles, dalmatians resemble a number of other short-haired dogs, including beagles and labrador retrievers. It's the distinctive black spots scattered all over a pure white coat that sets them apart.

What You'll Need

- DecoArt Patio Paint in Cloud White, Wrought Iron Black, Geranium Red, Patio Brick
- assorted stiff, flat craft brushes
- Loew-Cornell script liner, no. 1
- graphite pencil
- spray acrylic sealer

1 Choose a rock.

Look for a plump rock at least 3" high (7.5cm) with a flat bottom. One side should feature an outward slope to accommodate the haunch and rear leg. A slope on the opposite side could provide space for the front paws to sprawl, but if your rock features a blunt end as mine does, you can simply tuck those front paws in under the head.

When the bottom portion of a rock curves inward, it's hard to make paws that will show, so save those rocks for something else. The surface where the head will go should be fairly smooth, while the area for the haunch may have imperfections as mine does (a small crease in the rock). If a flaw is deep or distracting, use a bit of wood filler to fill in or smooth it over.

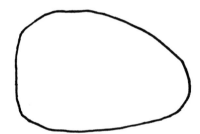

possible layouts for various rocks

2 Lay out the head.

Often I basecoat the rock first, then sketch on the design. Another option is to sketch the features first, then paint around them, leaving narrow lines uncovered to define the animal. Begin with a square head shape that takes up nearly a third of the front surface of your rock. My rock measures 6½" (16.5cm) from end to end, and my head square is 2½" (6.5cm) across. Bisect the head square horizontally. Divide the lower half in half again with a second horizontal line. Along this lower line sketch in a smaller square muzzle equal in size to one quarter of the head square. Instead of centering the muzzle, set it so that between two-thirds and three-fourths of the muzzle is to one side of the head's vertical midline, with the remaining portion on the other side. Sketch in an oval nose, setting it evenly between the side of the muzzle and the head's vertical midline.

Either freehand or using a straight edge, extend the side lines of the muzzle square up to intersect with the head's horizontal midline. Center the dog's eyes at those intersecting points. To form the bridge of the nose, angle lines from the top corners of the muzzle square to the inside edges of the eyes above. Round out the sides and bottom of the muzzle square as shown. Extend a line from the center of the nose downward to divide the muzzle, curving mouth lines off in either direction. Round off the lower half of the head square by angling lines from the middles of either side of the muzzle over to the sides of the head, cutting off the sharp corners.

From the inside corner of the eye positioned closest to the edge of the head square, extend a line straight up to the top of the head and begin one ear there. Create a line that curves up slightly from the head until it is just past the top corner of the head, then drop it down at nearly a right angle to parallel the side of the face. Stop when it is about even with the nose. Give the tip of the ear a sharp point, then bring the inside edge of the ear back up to the starting point, adding a slight outward curve to what would otherwise be an almost triangular shape. Since the dog's head is slightly turned, begin the second ear not above the second eye, but over almost to the corner of that opposite side. Slant the top of the ear down as you extend it beyond the head square until it ends level with or slightly below the tip of the first ear. Curve the inside of the ear toward the head as you bring it back up, shaving down some of the space between the eye and the original edge of the face.

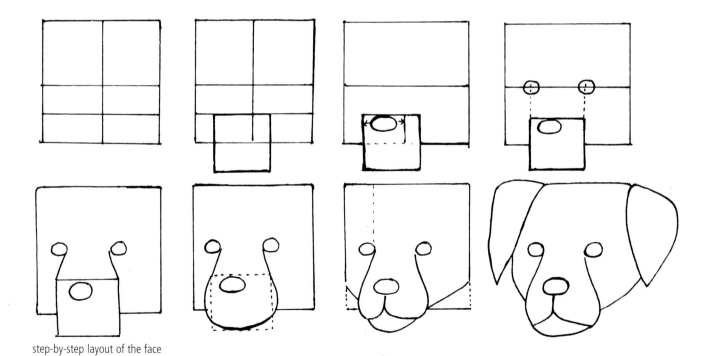

step-by-step layout of the face

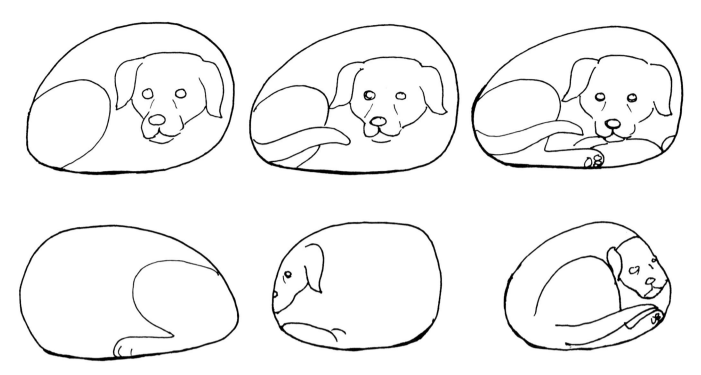

step-by-step layout of the body

3 Lay out the body.

Once the head is done, the remaining components are relatively uncomplicated. Move to the opposite end of the rock and create an oval haunch similar in size to the head, placed lengthwise. Curve a tail in from just beyond the bottom of the haunch, allowing it to angle up then droop down as it tapers to a rounded end. Fit a rear leg below the tail, shaped somewhat like an **L**, with a set of small oval pads showing on the paw. Use the space remaining between head and haunch to suggest a crease in the upper front leg. Give the lower leg a slight angle so that it seems to rise slightly below the head before it curves to end with a blunt paw. Bring the other front leg in from the far side like a long oval, so that the two paws almost touch near the end of the rock. Very little will show on the rear side of your rock, save for a crescent of back hip corresponding to the front one.

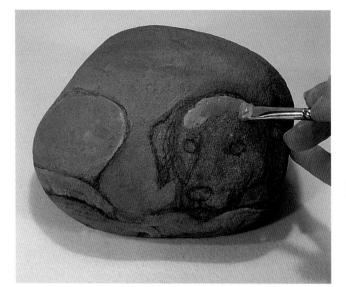

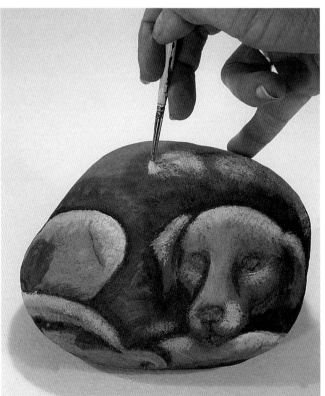

4 Paint the basecoat.

Mix one part black paint to two parts white for a medium shade of gray and use a small, stiff flat brush to cover the surface of the rock, careful not to go over the guidelines. Make sure you paint all the way to the base of the rock so that no unpainted edges show. I missed filling in the chin when applying this coat and had to do so later.

5 Create dimension with shadows.

Use the same brush and deeper gray (three parts black to one part white) to shade areas that should appear to recede, like the midsection between the head and haunch, the areas surrounding the legs and all around the head. Turn your flat brush sideways to stroke in the shadowed line running along the defining edge of the muzzle, with a shorter shadow on the corresponding side. Keep your brush rather dry by stroking excess paint onto your newspaper. Drybrushing will give your dark shadows a soft, diffused look. When shading the area beneath the muzzle, use an even darker gray—almost black—to suggest more depth and provide extra contrast for the head. On the back side of the rock you will need only to shade around the partial hip showing there. Make the tail stand out by giving it a narrow line of shadow above and below where it overlaps the haunch.

6 Add highlights.

You may use the same brush or one slightly smaller to heighten the illusion of dimension with white highlights. Again go for a diffused look, keeping your brush dry and lightly loaded. The areas that need highlighting are those that would catch light naturally; the top of the head and tops of the ears, the cheekbones below the eyes, on the muzzle at either side of the nose leather. Also, highlight the top curve of both haunches, the upper half of the tail, and the upper half of the front legs (except where the head shades a portion). Add another small smudge of highlighting to accentuate the crease above the base of the front leg. Other areas to highlight include the shoulders curving gently just beyond the shading behind the head. This area should form a soft **M** shape. Skip a space and make a second, matching swath behind the shoulders.

7 Define the facial features.

Switch to a script liner brush and mix up a tiny amount of pale pink by adding just a tip-full of Geranium Red paint to a larger drop of white. Use this color to add a sparse mustache of pink to the muzzle area directly below the nose. Rinse your brush and use straight black, loosened as needed with water, to fill in the nose leather. Outline the shape of the mouth and the eye circles, too, adding small corners at the lower inside and upper outside points. For the eyes, darken a tiny drop of Patio Brick with just enough black to create a dark, chocolate brown and use this to fill in both eye circles.

8 Add the spots.

Use a small round or worn-down flat brush to begin dappling your dog with its pattern of spots. Avoid symmetry by placing some spots in random clusters of twos and threes. Start at the head with smaller spots that vary in shape and size. Make the ear spots larger, perhaps even partially covering one of the ears. Then, work your way backwards, adding spots in the shadowed areas as well as along the highlighted features. Try to let the shape of the spots suggest the shape of the underlying body parts, so that they seem to curve slightly where the dog's haunch is curved, or are partially hidden from view atop the dog's head.

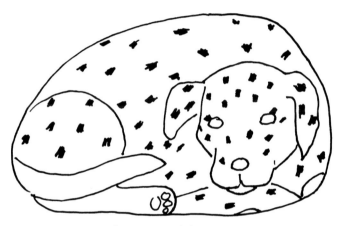

these spots are too uniform in size and placement

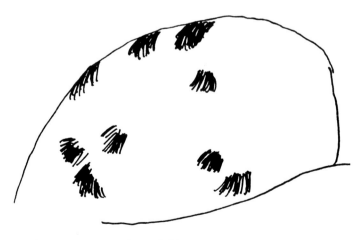

these spots correspond to underlying contours

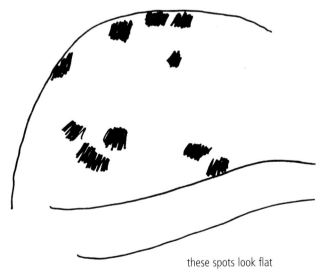

these spots look flat

How to Paint a Dalmatian

9 Create fur texture.

At this point your Dalmatian is still more black and gray than black and white, but against a darker background, short, white fur will stand out more clearly than white-on-white fur would. To make the delicate, splinter strokes for short fur, you will need to adjust the consistency of your paint. Add small increments of water to white paint and mix until it is loose enough to flow smoothly off the tip of your script liner brush, without running or turning transparent as it dries. Test strokes on newspaper will help you check for the right balance of paint and water. Also, holding your brush almost perpendicular to the surface and using just the tip will keep your fur crisply defined. Begin by detailing the sides of the face with the shortest and most delicate of strokes set as closely together as you can make them. Accent the eyes by encircling them with white outlines just beyond the black ones, and give the chin a fringe of fur. Next fill in the interior of the face with more layers of small strokes, following the fur direction guide. Avoid obliterating the darker lines defining the muzzle or the bridge of the nose. Interior fur strokes need not be as dense as those used along the outer edges, but they should still be short and delicate, and done in overlapping layers for a seamless look. On the ears, the fur should be densest at the tops and more sparse along the lower portions. Remember that fur tends to grow outward away from the nose, so when you reach a black spot, detail it with a fringe of white fur along the edge closest to the nose. Later you can detail the far sides of the spots with black fur strokes.

In areas that are deeply shadowed, allow more distance between each fur stroke so that the overall impression of shadowing still shows through under a light layer of fur. For areas that should be lighter, like the upper bridge of the nose, your strokes can be so close and dense as to nearly appear solid white. Along the muzzle, stroke sideways to suggest several rows of whisker follicles there.

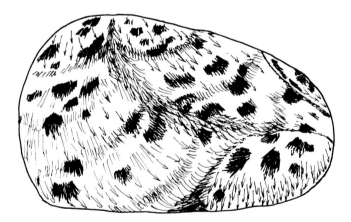

fur direction guide

10 Detail the haunch.

As with the face, begin by outlining the entire outer edge with very dense splinter strokes, then fill in the interior, again clustering more strokes in highlighted areas while making them sparser as you work down into the shadowed areas. Add a fringe of texture to the sides of the spots indicating the direction the fur is growing, which on the haunch would be the top side.

11 Detail the shoulders and back.

To detail the shoulders and backside, it's helpful to turn the rock so you can stroke toward yourself rather than away. Concentrate your strokes in those areas you previously highlighted, spacing the strokes farther apart in shadowy areas before dwindling away altogether to leave a dark margin for contrast. Detail the spots along the sides facing the head. Now move down, curving your sets of strokes in wide crescents to suggest the gentle curve of the dog's body in the direction of the tail. This curving is also reflected in the changing direction of the detailing fringe along the edge of the spots, so consult the fur direction illustration for guidance. Remember to make your fur lines more sparse as you near the bottom edge of the rock where it would naturally be more shadowed. Leave a darker spine line in place down the center of the back.

12 Complete the fur.

Turn your rock around again, and work on detailing the remaining unfinished areas. The fur surrounding the head tends to radiate out from it like sunrays. Don't stroke too far into the shadowy margins needed to set off the head and define other elements such as that small crease above the base of the front leg. To give the chest a bit more volume, add an extra dense few rows of strokes surrounding the face just beyond the ear.

Next move to the front leg, making the fur very short and dense along the top edge, except where the head overlaps it. Handle the tail in a similar fashion, leaving the bottom half mostly shaded. The rear leg is also detailed mainly along the top, with the fur becoming sparser in the middle with only a bit of broken line along the bottom edge.

13 Detail the nose.

To give the nose detail and dimension, add two white, C-shaped nostril holes like reversed parentheses. Soften the white paint to pale gray and create a gleam across the top of the nose just below the edge.

14 Detail the eyes.

I used black paint to tidy up the outer eye, then reapplied the white outline and gave the inside eye a tiny corner of white. To complete the eyes, use straight black paint to create an oval shaped pupil near the top of each eye. With a tiny amount of Patio Brick on the brush tip, add a narrow crescent of reddish-brown inside the bottom half of each eye. One or two white dots in the pupils will give your dalmatian's eyes a lifelike gleam.

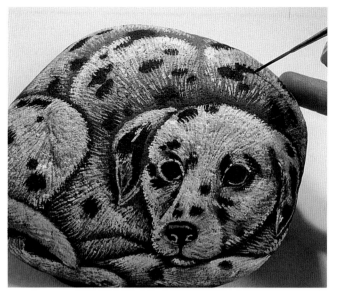

15 Detail the spots.
I used black to add touches of fringe to the backsides of my spots wherever I thought they needed the extra definition.

16 Finish paws.
Making the rear foot's paw pads pink would adds a welcome bit of color to the piece. Mix a touch of red into a drop of white paint and fill in the centers of each individual pad, leaving a border of gray surrounding them.

17 Finish the tail.
In looking over my dog, I felt that the tail needed more definition, so I used dark gray to stroke in some additional fur texture just where the tail overlaps the haunch. Work at training your eye to see areas that are not clearly defined or that lack needed contrast. Developing that judgment is part of your ongoing growth as an artist.

Painting Pets on Rocks

How to Paint an
Irish Setter

An Irish setter's rich russet coat, splashed with fiery highlights, makes this dog a striking subject. Changing coat colors will allow you to paint other kinds of setters as well. With minor modifications you can also create golden retrievers, cocker spaniels, collies and a host of other long-haired dogs. Rendering the flowing or feathery coat of a long-haired dog requires a slightly different technique than that used for short-haired dogs.

What You'll Need

- DecoArt Patio Paint in Geranium Red, Wrought Iron Black, Patio Brick, Sunshine Yellow, Sunflower Yellow, Cloud White
- assorted stiff, flat brushes
- no. 4 or 6 round brush
- 1/4" Silver Brush Ruby Satin Grass Comb
- Loew-Cornell script liner, no. 1
- white charcoal pencil
- spray acrylic sealer

1 Choose a rock.

When selecting a rock, look for a plump oval, preferably with a slight angle at one end suggesting the crook of the rear leg. Your rock can be fairly high, almost loaf-shaped or merely rounded on top. The rock I selected is 7" (18cm) long, 5" (12.5cm) across and just under 3" (7.5cm) high. If my rock had a side that was flat enough to stand up on, I could have opted for a more upright pose, but avoid rocks so tall and round that your dog will seem to be arching its back. Scrub your rock and allow it to dry. Sketching the dog's features on in pencil is a good way to experiment and see how best to fit them to your particular rock.

2 Paint the basecoat.

Mix up enough paint to cover the entire visible surface of your rock, using two parts Geranium Red to one part black to get a very deep reddish-brown. Apply with a large flat brush, slightly dampened. Allow the paint to dry.

two parts red, one part black (Irish setter basecoat)

black with a trace of red

two parts Sunshine Yellow, one part Patio Brick and one part red

two parts Sunshine Yellow and one part Patio Brick

two parts red and one part Patio Brick

Sunflower Yellow

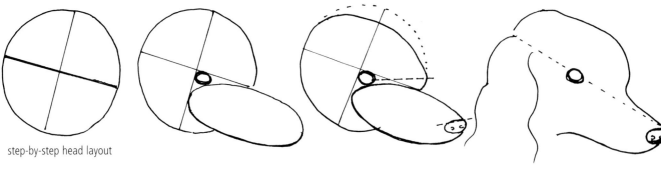

step-by-step head layout

3 Sketch the features.

Because setters have drooping ears, head placement can be higher on the rock as though the dog's head is raised. Consider how much space your rock has for the ear, which will splay out at the end if the head is low. My rock's side curves in slightly near the base, making a splayed ear difficult to render, so I opted for a slightly raised head. With a white charcoal pencil, sketch a circle for the head. This circle should be placed to one side of the rock, but with room beyond the outside edge to fit the ear. On my 7" (18cm) rock, the head circle measures 2½" (6.5cm), or approximately one-third of the rock's length. In this case, the head is tilted down, so I bisected the head circle with a line that slants toward the center of the rock. I then bisected the rock in the opposite direction, forming a cross. The muzzle is a large, elongated oval. Begin the oval in the lower inside quarter of the head circle and extend it until equal parts are inside and outside of the head. The muzzle's length should be the same as the diameter of the head and wide enough to nearly fill the space of that quarter. Fit the eye into the center corner of that same quarter. A straight line from the eye circle to a corresponding point just above where the top of the muzzle oval crosses the head circle indicates where a second, unseen eye would be. Use this same straight line as a guide while sketching a small oval nose into the upper end of the muzzle. The top of the nose oval should be set on a line parallel to that of the eyes above it. This will help you avoid a skewed look. The same point where the eye line crosses the head circle also indicates where to begin modifying the head shape. Just above the unseen eye, shave off the entire top curve so that the head is flattened. For a cocker spaniel, leave the head a rounded dome. Add the ear, beginning inside the head circle at a point that lines up with the top of the nose and the center of the eye circle. From the base of the ear allow the outermost ear line to gently curve out and away from the head as the fur flows gracefully downward. My dog's ear measures ¾" (2cm) across the top.

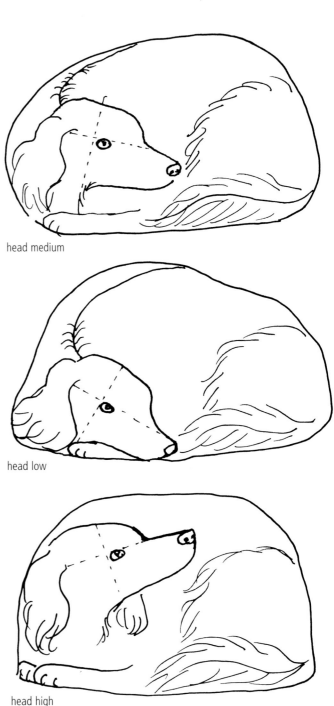

head medium

head low

head high

4 Finish the layout.

To complete your layout, bring a sweeping plume of a tail in from the base at the opposite end of the rock, allowing the tip to taper off below the dog's head. Add a narrow front leg that begins where the tail tip ends, fitting the paw below the chest. Sketch a spine line that curves out from behind the head just above the base of the ear. Allow this spine line to follow the contour of your rock until it ends at the base of the tail. Above the tail, indicate the curve of a haunch similar in size to the head (measured from nose to base of ear). Look your sketch over to see how all the elements fit together. Double-check to ensure that the nose and eyes are parallel.

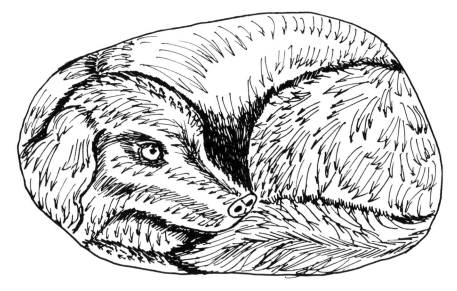

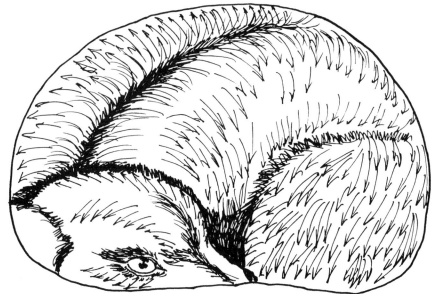

fur direction guide

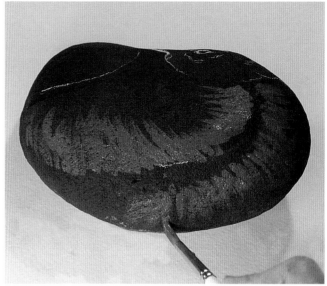

5 Create contours with shading.

For dimension and depth, use black paint, softened with just a trace amount of Geranium Red, to darken the areas surrounding the head, haunch, and the space between these two features. Go around the tail, ear and down the spine. Use a round brush or the side of a flat one to feather out the edges of your shadows, avoiding harsh contrasts. Shade the center portion of the setter's tail to indicate a natural part in the fur there.

6 Heighten the contours with highlights.

Highlights suggest the dramatic play of light over the dog's fur, emphasizing the shape of features and adding subtle texture. Again using a round brush, the side of a flat one, or a grass comb for the larger areas, mix two parts Sunshine Yellow with one part red and one part Patio Brick. Add just enough water to ensure smooth application. Begin on the backside, stroking a line of curving highlights along either side of the darkened spine line. Nestle each stroke up against the previous one, but allow them to separate as they taper to points. These strokes should grow longer as you proceed toward the tail end. Consult the fur direction guide, and end the strokes well before reaching the top of the haunch. Leave the dog's midsection mostly dark for now.

Turn your rock around and use slightly more diluted paint to suggest a silkier sheen along the top of the head. Leave the center of the muzzle dark all the way up between the eyes and into the forehead. Add a softly blended line of highlighting just below this dark swath, moving first over the top of the eye, then down and around the bottom to encircle it, while leaving a dark oval of basecoat surrounding the eye itself. Return to more concentrated paint to suggest several layers of fur flowing like ripples down the ear. Use the tip of your brush to create a series of short ragged lines along the jaw line and neck.

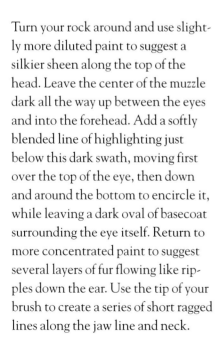

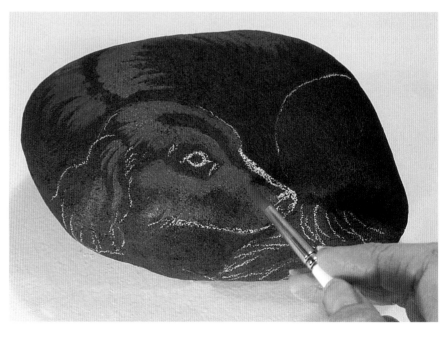

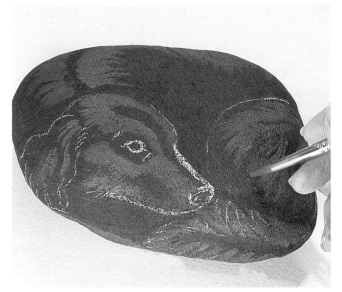

Softly highlight along the top of the front leg. Add highlights along the tail similar to those made along either side of the spine line. More feathery strokes add detail to the haunch. Concentrate them just below the top curve, then scatter them more randomly, but in the direction the fur would naturally flow as indicated by the fur direction guide.

7 Outline the eyes and nose.
While the highlights are drying, switch to a script liner and black paint to outline around the nose, fill in the nostrils and outline the eye.

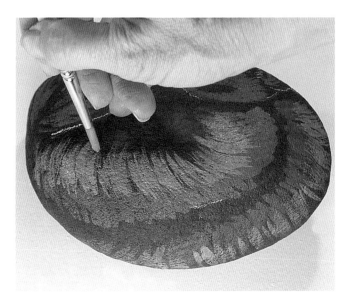

8 Add a layer of light and texture.
Mix two parts Sunshine Yellow with one part Patio brick to create a tone visibly brighter than the previous color. Use the tip of your round brush or a grass comb to create an overlapping, somewhat ragged row of strokes that begin where your first set of spine highlights left off, again allowing the tips of the strokes to separate. Try for a more soft, diffused look, holding your brush perpendicular to the surface.

From there, concentrate lighter strokes along the top half of the tail and then the haunch in a rather random fashion. Do more highlighting on the ear, mainly around the top where light would fall first. Add a narrow line of pale golden color to the very top of the muzzle to make it stand out. Continue along the top of the head, using the lighter tone to visually set the head off from the body.

How to Paint an Irish Setter

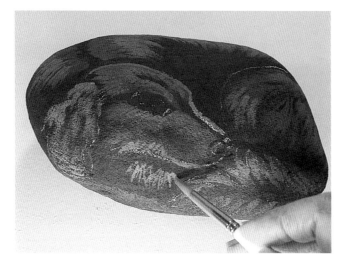

Similarly, bring out the jaw line by blending a ragged row of fur into the darker highlights there. Make a smoother outline along the bottom of the muzzle ending near the nose. To keep the area directly below the head from seeming bottomless, add a ruff of coarse fur to the center, leaving the surrounding edges of the area dark.

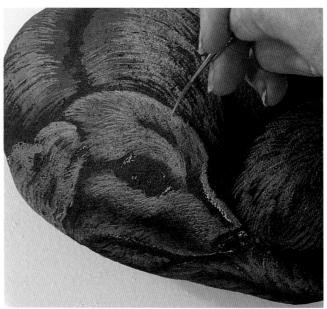

9 Add delicate fur details.
Continuing with the same color, switch to your script liner brush (or, if your rock is smooth, try using your grass comb) to create clusters of fur lines that are dense, but thin and much more delicate than those previously done. Adjust the consistency of your paint so that it is almost like ink. Leave a margin of darker basecoat showing, then drop down below the second set of highlighting strokes along the dog's midsection between head and haunch. Note how narrow, yet distinct, dark margins around all main features help to define them. As you add these longer, more delicate lines, curve them in small clusters that suggest waviness. Allow some lines to cross others here and there. Move next to the top and side of the haunch, concentrating these fine fur lines to emulate the way light would fall on the curved roundness of the haunch. Make fewer and more sparse strokes in the lower portions.

On the head, use your script liner brush to create much shorter and more dense fur, adding texture and light to the top of the head, to the highlighted parts of the muzzle, and around the eyes, jaw line and ear. Along the muzzle in particular, make overlapping rows of short splinter strokes rather than longer ones. A fringe of short, diagonal lines along the inside edge of the ear near the top is another nice detail.

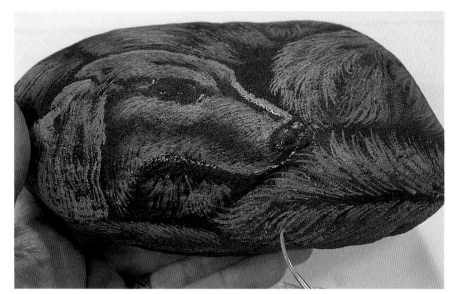

Along the top of the front leg, create a series of very short, very uniform strokes, like a slanted row of splinters whose tips show up dramatically against the dark basecoat above. On the tail, these lines add realistic texture and visual interest, but use them sparingly so that the subtle interplay of previous layers of color show through.

10 Accent the highlights.

Now mix one part Patio Brick with two parts red and, still using a script liner, go back over your animal's coat, adding a scattering of this deeper reddish-brown to both complement and accent the lighter highlights. Use them to soften and blend the areas where darker and lighter fur strokes adjoin, such as along the spine. In the space below the head, the lighter ruff looks a bit stark against the dark basecoat. Deep red fur lines can create a more natural transition. Other places to use it include the dark oval surrounding the eye, down the center line of the muzzle and in the middle of the forehead. Avoid diminishing the highlights by keeping these red strokes very sparse.

11 Fill in the eyes.

Mix Patio Brick and Sunshine Yellow to get a warm golden brown. Use this and your script liner brush to fill in the eye circle, leaving the center dark. Add a touch of black to your eye color and create a small crescent of shadow within the top half of the eye. When dry, add an oval, black pupil that hangs from the top of the eye.

12 Detail the eyes and nose.

Add a bit of black to a drop of white paint to make a soft gray, and underline the bottom half of the eye just outside its black outline. Deepen this gray with more black and add a tiny amount of red to create the dark pink-ish-gray tone of the nose leather. Use it to surround each nostril, leaving a dark line between them. Then, add white to make a highlighting color and use the very tip of your liner to create a narrow half circle gleam above and below each nostril.

13 Detail the coat with yellow.

In looking over my dog's coat, I determined that it could use one more layer of highlighting to heighten the look of shimmering fire. I used straight Sunflower Yellow and my script liner to sprinkle a few bright touches among the areas previously highlighted. It's easy to overlook places that are tucked out of the way, like the front leg, but highlighting the fur along the top really helps define it.

The addition of one or two white dots to the eye gives your painted dog the look of a live dog suddenly watching you.

Painting Pets on Rocks

How to Paint a
Bulldog

Bulldogs, pugs, Boston terriers and Pekingese may not win conventional beauty contests, but to their devotees these stout little canines have charms that far outweigh their homeliness. Often they are described as being so ugly they're cute.

For rock painters, the obvious advantage is that, with no muzzle to speak of, bulldogs and other flat-faced dogs fit easily onto an array of rock shapes, most particularly round rocks that are not suitable for most other subjects.

What You'll Need

- DecoArt Patio Paint in Pinecone Brown, Wrought Iron Black, Cloud White, Patio Brick, Sunflower Yellow, Geranium Red
- assorted stiff, flat brushes and smaller brushes for shading
- a scruffy flat brush or Silver Brush Ruby Satin Grass Comb
- Loew-Cornell script liner, no. 1
- white charcoal pencil
- spray acrylic sealer

1 Choose a rock.

When selecting your rock, look for chubby ones that are circular or oval, but with one flatter side to serve as the base. Rounded rocks with a higher profile can be employed for sitting poses. The most important consideration is a broad area where the face, with its generous jowls, dewlaps and widely spaced eyes, will fit. The hindquarters seem petite by comparison, so if your round rock tapers at one end, so much the better. The rock I selected is fairly uniform, yet not perfectly round, and about the size of a small melon. From end to end it measures 7" (18cm) and it is 5¹/₂" (14cm) wide. The end I chose for the head had a small crack slightly off center that I filled in with a bit of wood filler.

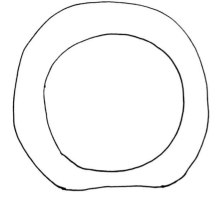
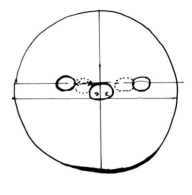

step-by-step head layout

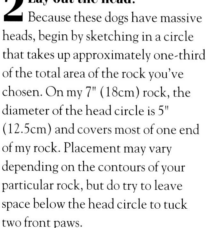

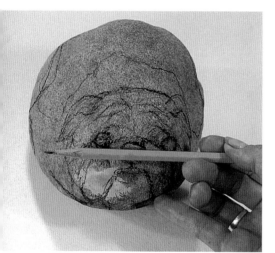

2 Lay out the head.

Because these dogs have massive heads, begin by sketching in a circle that takes up approximately one-third of the total area of the rock you've chosen. On my 7" (18cm) rock, the diameter of the head circle is 5" (12.5cm) and covers most of one end of my rock. Placement may vary depending on the contours of your particular rock, but do try to leave space below the head circle to tuck two front paws.

Bisect the head circle both horizontally and vertically, then place an oval nose so that it is in the center resting atop the horizontal midline. Next make a second horizontal line that runs across the top of the nose oval. Center the eye circles on this line, with a space equal to the diameter of an eye circle between it and the nose.

Below the nose, extend a short line down the vertical bisecting line, then split it into two diverging mouth lines that curve sharply sideways until each

is well past being even with the outside edge of the nose oval. Curve the mouth lines downward from there, angling them slightly away from each other. When you reach the bottom edge of the head circle, form a curved jowl. Depending on your rock, these jowls may even droop slightly beyond the head circle. They should then loop back up and run parallel to the inside mouth/jowl lines, before curving in just below the eye circles to join above the nose oval.

The ears are small flaps slightly indented into the head circle and set so that the base of either ear lines up with the outside edge of the eye below. Make a **J**-shaped line curving out beyond the head circle and dropping down along side it until the tip is even with the first horizontal bisecting line.

Go back to the mouth lines below the nose and indicate a bottom lip below them. Holding a pencil level with the eyes is a simple way to check for symmetry.

Painting Pets on Rocks

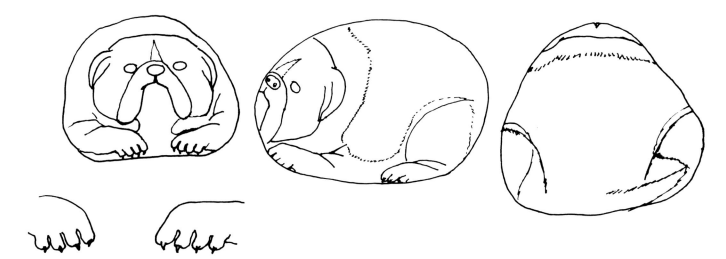

3 Layout the body.

Below the jowls, leave a small open space. Then, sketch in two stubby round paws at the ends of equally stubby legs curving in from either side. Fit the ends of the paws with a set of four oval toes and four pointy little toenails. Turn your rock sideways and create an elbow and short upper leg as shown. At the rear of the rock on either side, create a round haunch that is one-third to one-half the size of the head, with elongated back paws extending from the bottom. Finish the feet by adding three small curving toes. The tail can either be a short, docked stub or a thick, tapered tail that curves off to one side. That completes your basic layout.

4 Paint the brown patches.

Markings vary from dog to dog, and color patches range from dark blond to deep brown to brindle and every shade in between. My choice is a medium shade of brown concentrated in a saddle shape on the back and sides, along with the upper half of the head. Use Pinecone Brown and a large flat brush to cover the back, sides and rear portion of the haunches. I also left a narrow space around the front of each haunch to be painted white along with the bottom of the midsection surrounding the rear feet. Paint the top of the head, leaving a narrow blaze unpainted above the nose.

How to Paint a Bulldog

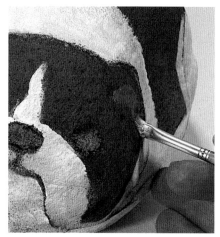

6 Fill in the ears.
Mix a tiny amount of red into white paint to get a medium shade of pink. Add just a touch of black to soften the pink to a dusky shade and use this to paint the insides of the ears.

7 Paint the facial features.
Switch to black paint and a script liner to outline the nose, mouth/jowl and eyes. Fill in the entire space above the bottom lip, then add enough water to your paint to thin it almost to transparency, and stroke a ragged row of vertical lines below the bottom lip to a little beyond halfway to the bottoms of the jowls.

8 Add some facial details.
Mix enough black into Patio Brick to get a dark chocolate brown. Use a script liner to go around the outlines of the jowls with tiny splinter strokes. Change the angles of these strokes in relation to the nose—they should radiate out like sunrays. Create the same delicate fringe around the ear edges to define their shapes in a furry way.

9 Define the features with outlines.
For a bolder outline that also can be accomplished more quickly, select a stiff, flat craft brush. Add water to your dark brown mixture and do some short test strokes that are little more than pressing the brush down then picking it up again with only enough drag to create the suggestion of texture. Repeat this stroke in a line along the top of the head, then skip down to the edges of the face and do the same, always pulling your brush away from the line you're emphasizing.

Use scant paint and a dry brush to scrub black paint into smudgy shadows below the jowls.

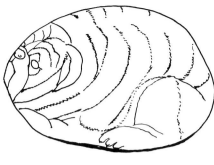
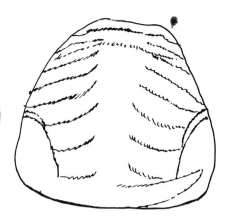

placement of dewlaps, wrinkles and folds

10 Paint some wrinkles and folds.

Add a small amount of Patio Brick to your black paint. Between the eyes, create two short, curved lines that begin above either side of the nose and end by curving into the eye circles halfway across. Make a second set of parallel curves that begin inside the first set and end beyond the outside corner of either eye. Another set of wrinkles start near the bottom of the jowl on either side and curve up to below the ear. These end in the center of the forehead. Make two more shorter wrinkles, one below and one above the ones you just made. Indicate a small, sagging line under either eye. Between the jowls and front paws, paint in a pair of curved dewlaps.

11 Complete the remaining outlines.

Go over the leg outlines and creases. Create a series of wrinkles or fold lines around the head and along the sides. Break off those nearest the head before they meet at the top of the back. Also, go around the haunch, rear leg and foot.

From the rear, outline the tail as it curves around one side, or outline the stub if the tail is docked.

How to Paint a Bulldog

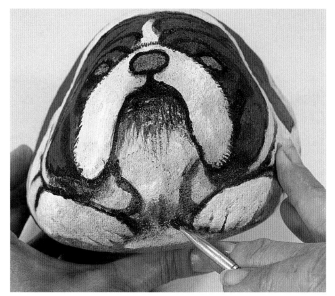

12 Shadow dewlaps and paws.
Use black and a dry brush to create shadows below the dew laps and between paws.

13 Highlight the brown folds.
Mix Pinecone Brown and Sunflower Yellow to get a warm blond color. Use a stiff, flat brush and keep it dry, applying paint along the tops of the folds then scrubbing it into the middles for a soft, diffused look.

Do the same soft highlighting along the tops of the folds along the dog's backside, blending the lighter color into the darker basecoat. Highlight along the top side of the tail, too.

14 Detail the white patch behind the head.
Mix white and black paint to get a medium gray. Loosen with water and use your script liner to make a fringe of gray fur lines behind the head. Keep your strokes delicate but dense, and intersperse with longer strokes. Work all the way around the head, keeping these fur lines perpendicular to the line they are shadowing. When the head is done, detail any folds in the white patch behind the head.

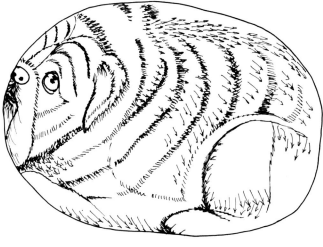

fur direction guide

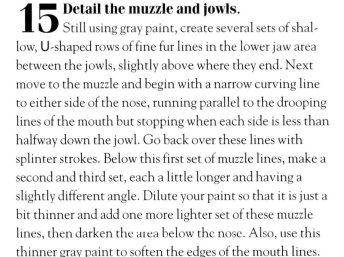

15 Detail the muzzle and jowls.

Still using gray paint, create several sets of shallow, U-shaped rows of fine fur lines in the lower jaw area between the jowls, slightly above where they end. Next move to the muzzle and begin with a narrow curving line to either side of the nose, running parallel to the drooping lines of the mouth but stopping when each side is less than halfway down the jowl. Go back over these lines with splinter strokes. Below this first set of muzzle lines, make a second and third set, each a little longer and having a slightly different angle. Dilute your paint so that it is just a bit thinner and add one more lighter set of these muzzle lines, then darken the area below the nose. Also, use this thinner gray paint to soften the edges of the mouth lines.

16 Add details to white areas.

Adding realistic details to all the remaining white areas can be done in two basic steps. First, use delicate gray fur lines to create the look of shadows on the lower sides of any feature. This means along the bottom curve of the front legs, along the lower edge of the rear legs, the lower edges of the haunches and along the bottom of any space showing between the rear paw and the front leg. Use lighter gray strokes to suggest milder shadows where one feature might overlap another, such as below the head or along the lower edges of the white folds. When you've completed this shadowing, switch to white paint that's been loosened enough to create delicate details, and begin adding a fringe of white fur to any edge where white fur meets brown.

How to Paint a Bulldog

17 **Add details to the brown areas.**
In the same way, but with a different color, add fur texture to the folds and wrinkles in your dog's brown areas. Mix enough Sunflower Yellow into your white paint to get a discernibly lighter shade. Use your script liner and your most delicate fur strokes to add texture to the areas previously highlighted. Begin with the head, detailing not only the top edges of the folds, but also the outside edges of the head and the angles of the ears.

18 **Soften the edges further.**
When the head is completed, move on to the rest of the body, using your highlighting fur lines to further soften the edges where lighter color was scrubbed on earlier, as well as to give the back portions the look of real fur. Don't overlook the brown portions of the haunches or the top half of the tail.

19 **Integrate the fur lines on the spine.**
Mix up another small batch of dark brown by adding a brushful of black to a puddle of Patio Brick. Use this deeper brown to further integrate the fur lines along the back. Concentrate on the layers of fur down the center of the back where the spine runs to the base of the tail. Next, use these dark strokes to soften the edges of the folds along both sides of the back plus those that run down into the midsections between front and rear legs.

Once the back is completed, move to the face and use these dark fur lines to soften the face folds and wrinkles.

Painting Pets on Rocks

Enter to win a FREE handpainted rock from Lin Wellford, the original "rock artist!"

Nobody captures the spirit and personality of animals on rocks like Lin Wellford.

Here's your chance to have her paint one just for you! Simply fill out the information requested below and mail it to us at:

North Light Books
Attn: Rock Promotion
1507 Dana Avenue
Cincinnati, Ohio 45207

The editors of North Light Books will randomly select three winners from all entries received by October 31, 2001. If yours is chosen, you win! Lin Wellford will paint the pet of your choice (dog, cat, fish or bird) on a rock for you to keep, valued at $100! It's a one-of-a-kind gift that will last a lifetime. So what are you waiting for?

Also check out the back for a money-saving offer on other new craft titles!

HEY LIN, I WANT TO WIN!

NAME _____

ADDRESS _____

CITY _____ STATE _____ ZIP _____

PHONE _____ EMAIL_____

Enter today!

Get $3 OFF these select titles!

Simply mail in your original sales receipt for any one of the titles above, along with the <u>completed</u> **"HEY LIN, I WANT TO WIN!"** entry form on the reverse of this card and you'll receive $3!

*Offer not good with any other discount or book club purchase.
*Offer expires on October 31, 2001.

20 **Detail the eyes and nose.**
Fill in the eye circles with straight Pinecone Brown, then add a crescent of Sunflower Yellow to the lower half of each eye as a highlight. While the eyes are drying, color in the nose leather with solid black.

21 **Finish the eyes, nose and mouth.**
Now add a black pupil to the upper center of each eye. Mix up a paler shade of gray, and use this on your script liner to create a gleam across the top of the nose and a pair of half-round nostrils. Also, use this gray to paint in the barest suggestion of a gleam to the upper half of the lower lip, and a longer gleam along the bottom of the lower lip. Add a scattering of gray fur lines to the chin area, too. Then, with the very tip of your brush, make narrow curves of gray below each eye, letting the curves sag toward the outside edges to give the eyes a droopy look.

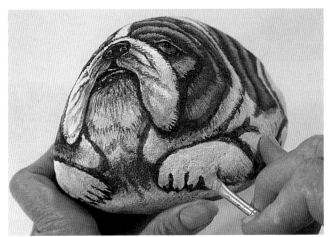

22 **Add the final touches.**
Small white gleams in each eye have a powerful impact on this piece. As an afterthought, I added a narrow defining line of lightened Sunflower Yellow to the eyelid to give the eyes a bit more emphasis.

In looking over my bulldog, I decided that adding a blush of pink to the front toes would be a nice touch. I mixed up a very pale shade of pink from Geranium Red and white and used a dry brush to simply scrub the color onto the toes. A light spray of sealer will make all your colors seem richer.

How to Paint a Bulldog

Painting Pets on Rocks

How to Paint a
Yorkie

Yorkshire terriers are among the most popular of those tiny dogs bred as lap pets. With their shoe-button eyes and lively dispositions, plus an elegant cascade of silky fur, it's easy to see why people find Yorkies irresistible companions.

Not surprisingly, rock Yorkies are adorable, too. To paint your own, look for tombstone-shaped rock that will stand up on a flat end. Yorkies can also be painted on narrow, loaf-shaped rocks.

1 Choose a rock.

The rock I found for this project stands just under 7" (18cm) high and tapers slightly at the top. Avoid rocks that are so pointy that the two ears at the top can not be at least one ear-width apart. Adequate height for upright ears is also an important consideration, and my rock, being rounded at the top and almost 4" (10cm)

thick, allows ample room for them, although the tips will lay across the top of the rock. This means my finished piece will look best when viewed from above. Yorkies' coats are often clipped into shorter layers, but those that participate in dog shows sport long, luxuriant show coats that flow down to the floor.

What You'll Need

- DecoArt Patio Paint in Wrought Iron Black, Cloud White, Sunflower Yellow, Patio Brick, Daisy Cream, Sunshine Yellow (or other bow color of your choice)
- assorted stiff, flat brushes including one ³/₄" or larger
- no. 4 or 6 round
- Silver Brush Ruby Satin Grass Comb (optional)
- Loew-Cornell script liner, no. 1
- graphite pencil
- Sharpie marker (optional)
- spray acrylic sealer

lots of ear room

minimal ear room

not enough ear room

2 Sketch the features.

Begin by determining how the triangular ears can best fit your rock. If your rock is very thin along the top, it may not be feasible to wrap the ears around the curve there. In that case, begin the base of the ears lower down, and fill the center between the two ears with a taller sprout of pulled-back facial hair gathered into a little bow. On thicker rocks there is more room to maneuver, and ears can begin closer to the top of the front surface.

On my 7" (18cm) tall rock, the head is a 3" (7.5cm) circle with the bases of the ears slightly indented within it. Bisect the head circle horizontally and fit a second, smaller circle for the muzzle into the lower half as shown. Bisect this muzzle circle horizontally, too, indicating a mouth line. Along this mouth line sketch in a small, curved bottom lip, and below that a slightly broader chin crescent. Halfway between the mouth line and the top of the muzzle circle, sketch in a small oval nose.

Place the eyes so they rest along the horizontal midline, two full eye widths apart. The dog's eyes should not be overly large. On my dog they measure barely 1/2" (13mm) across.

Imagine how the fur around the eyes would be drawn up into a bow between the ears. It would follow a straight line up from the nose, while fur above the eyes would have to curve around the base of the ears.

The fur surrounding the muzzle and below the eyes should flow in loose parallel lines along either side of that circle, curving in slightly below the chin, then continuing in wavy lines down to the base of the rock.

Turn your rock to the side and make wavy lines to indicate the outside edges of the dog's mane as it flows from behind (or above) the ears and downward somewhat parallel to the curves of the lines around and down from the muzzle.

Make wavy lines to indicate the outside edges of the dog's mane as it flows from behind (or above) the ears and downward somewhat parallel to the curves of the lines around and down from the muzzle.

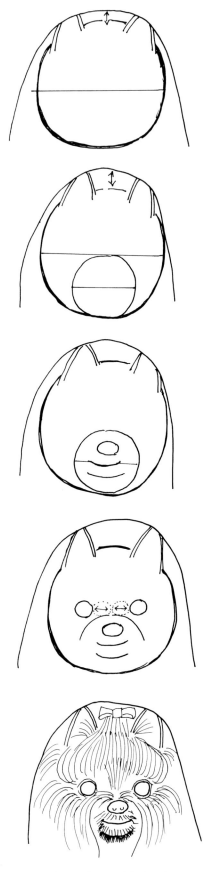

step-by-step layout of the head

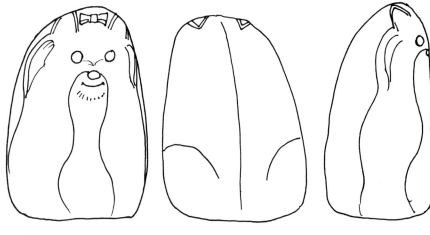

body layout

Painting Pets on Rocks

fur direction guide

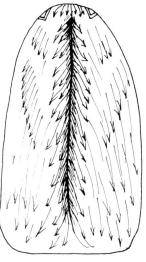

Here's my rock with the sketch in place.

color samples for mane

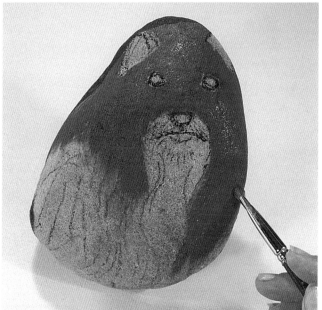

3 Paint the basecoat.

Use a large, flat brush and black paint to completely cover the back half of your rock, being careful to go around the tips of the ears if they protrude beyond the head. Paint all the way to the base of your rock so no uncovered surface can be seen.

4 Paint the mane.

To paint the mane, begin with a large puddle of Patio Brick and darken with just enough black paint to get a rich reddish-brown color. You may want to use a slightly smaller flat brush to apply this paint. Cover the entire mane area, leaving only the eyes, ears, the muzzle and the center of the chest below it unpainted.

How to Paint a Yorkie

Next, add even more black paint to your mixture, turning it into a deep, chocolate brown. Use this color to fill in the ear triangles as well as the muzzle and remaining chest area. If you're worried about covering over your mouth and chin lines, simply paint around them, or go over them with a sharpie marker that will show through all but the heaviest of paints.

Tilt your rock and add dark crescents along the very bottom to suggest the curved tops of two front paws peeking from below the fur there.

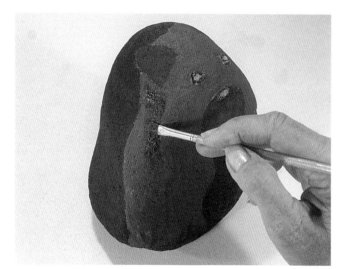

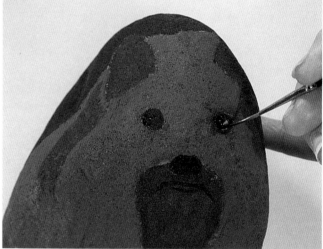

Finally, just below the ears along either side, paint a dark streak that follows the contours of the mane and tapers to a point that's level with the height of the chin.

5 Paint the facial features.
Switch to a script liner and straight black paint. Carefully outline around the shapes of the eyes, making them as round and symmetrical as you can. Also, outline and fill in the nose oval and paint over the mouth lines. Note how I added short slanting lines to either end of my upper mouth line.

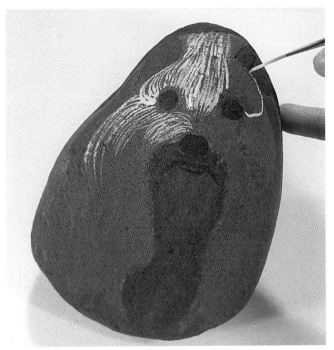

6 Create a flowing mane.

Combine white paint with enough Sunflower Yellow to make a pale, creamy gold. Add sufficient water to the paint so it will flow smoothly off the tip of your script liner, without being so watery that it runs or turns transparent. Leaving a narrow margin of basecoat in place, begin at the outside corner of either eye. Stroke in a set of narrow lines that curve out nearly as far as the outside edge of the ear, then circle back to run along the base of the ear to the inside corner, ending at the top of the head. Each successive line will be less curved as you work around the top of each eye. Between the eyes these lines should begin level with the bottoms of the eyes and extend up to the top of the head.

7 Detail the lower mane.

To detail the lower portion of the face and the rest of the flowing mane, start by making a curved row of lines along either side of the top of the muzzle. Leave a narrow margin between these muzzle lines and the row of lines beginning between the eyes above. In the same way, leave a narrow part showing down the center of the muzzle. Also, leave narrow margins of basecoat showing around the bottom edges of each eye as you surround them with fur strokes. The first few sets can be a few inches long, then begin pulling out longer lines that mirror the undulating curves of the mane all the way to the bottom of the rock. I made my lines denser at the tops of a curve, then sparser below, adding to the look of waviness. Keep my fur lines sparse over the dark shadows below either ear.

8 Detail below the nose and along the chest.

Lighten Patio Brick with a bit of Sunflower Yellow and use this color to add prickly texture to the lower portion of the muzzle. Surround the bottom half of the nose with short, bristling strokes, then make several layers of longer strokes to either side, following the shape of the mouth. Separate these strokes from the flowing fur of the mane. Skip down to the chest below the chin and make overlapping sets of long fur lines down until they feather out near the bottom. Again, leave margins of the darker basecoat undetailed to either side for contrast.

9 Outline the ears.
While you have this same reddish-gold color, use it to outline the edges of the ears, leaving narrow margins of darker color around the outlines wherever possible.

10 Outline the eyes.
Mix a tiny amount of black into Patio Brick to darken it, then add just enough white to get a creamy reddish-beige. Use this color to outline your eyes, leaving the inside lower corners open, and giving the outside upper edge a slight crimp. To further emphasize the eyes, mix some dark brown from Patio Brick and black, and go around the outside edges of the beige outlines.

11 Add more highlights.
Switch to Daisy Cream, again adjusting the texture of the paint by adding water until it flows smoothly without being too watery. Use this lighter color to complement and emphasize the fur lines surrounding the face and mane. Concentrate these strokes to suggest the play of light between and above the eyes and along the wavy curves of the mane, skipping over the more shaded areas. This will play up the contrast between lighter and darker fur. In particular, highlight the strands of fur along either side of the darker chest area, again to heighten contrast. Move to the bridge of the nose and, along either side of the darkened center, create pale, stiff fur that bristles up and out, with some delicate tips even arching up into the corners of the eyes.

12 Add details to the mouth and ears.

To a small amount of Daisy Cream, add a brushful of Patio Brick and another brushful of Sunflower Yellow. Use this light reddish-gold color and the very tip of your liner brush to fill in the narrow chin area below the mouth with very short, fine fur. Add a bit of water to loosen the paint, then use it to stroke in a cluster of ear whiskers that fan out from the inside corners.

13 Add contrasting strokes to the muzzle and chest.

Mix Patio Brick with black to get a dark brown color and, still using your script liner, stroke in delicate muzzle fur lines which radiate outward from the nose in short overlapping layers. Move down to the area below the chin and use shorter, denser strokes to suggest shading and create depth there. Scatter longer, sparser strokes down the chest area, also using them to heighten contrast along side the pale edges of the mane.

14 Tint the fur.

Add more Patio Brick to your mixture to make a reddish-brown color, then water it down until it is a transparent tint strong enough to color lighter areas but too weak to cover anything up. Use a medium-sized round or flat brush to apply this tint above and below the eyes so that the underlying texture of the fur still shows through, yet is softened. Note how this tinting is highest above the inside corner of the eye, then tapers toward the outside end, while underneath it is narrow along the inside corners, then widens before tapering off below the outside edges of the eyes.

15 Detail and emphasize the mane.

Next, stroke off excess tint onto a paper towel or newspaper. Scrub what remains on your brush into those areas of the mane not highlighted, to warm up and tone down the fur strokes and emphasize the look of waviness. Add a few strokes of this tint to the forehead, mostly near the top.

16 Finish the face.

Mix black and white to make a medium gray color. Use the tip of your script liner to make two small, half-round lines indicating nostrils in the lower half of the nose, then add a slightly curved gleam across the upper half. Make a very narrow line just above and parallel to the chin to suggest the gleam of a lower lip there. Rinse your brush well, then add small dots of light in the upper half of the eyes.

17 Finish the backside.

Switch to a larger stiff, flat brush, preferably one that's become slightly ragged with wear. You may want to experiment with a grass comb here. Mix black and white to make a medium to light shade of gray. Add enough water to allow the paint to flow smoothly, then apply clusters of strokes to the black fur along the back, following the diagram provided on page 117. Use slanted rows of strokes along either side of the spine to indicate that the fur divides along that line, then work out and down, leaving dark spaces between sets of soft gleams as well as between other features such as the rounded tops of the haunches and the area along the lighter mane on both sides.

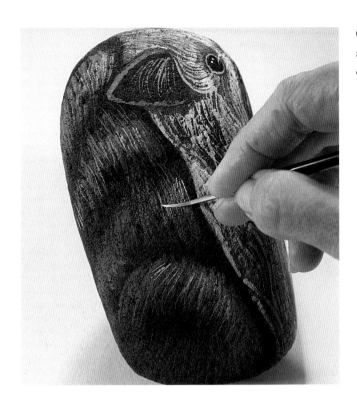

Go back with a much lighter gray and a script liner and add a row of lighter, more delicate fur lines to the upper center of each gleam to suggest more glossiness.

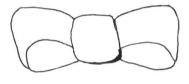

18 Add a bow.
Your bow can be any color you choose. I used Sunshine Yellow. Place the bow so that it nearly spans the space between the ears about halfway up. Fill in the bow shape with your base color. Darken your bow color with a touch of black and use this to outline the center knot and to indicate shadows below the top of the bow loops. Highlight the top edges of the loops and the top of the knot by adding a bit of white to the original color.

Seal your Yorkie and enjoy his winsome company for life.

More Ideas
Lap Dogs

This rock was nearly perfect for a Yorkie pup—I just built up the ears a bit with wood putty.

Pomeranians and Maltese are two more lap type dogs that seem made to order for rock painting.

This perky Scottie needed an unusual rock to accommodate his ears.

Poodle fur can be a challenge. Try applying it with a deerfoot stippler over a constrasting basecoat. For definition, add a small twist to each dabbing stroke.

Short-Haired Dogs

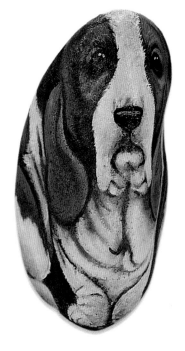

Can you see how the proportions differ between a pup and a full grown Labrador?

This rock practically begged me to turn it into a mournful Basset Hound.

Puppies grow up too quickly, so a rock pup like this Lab makes a wonderful souvenir of your dog's puppyhood.

Here's a napping Beagle.

Choose elongated rocks for dachshunds.

Long-Haired Dogs

Golden retrievers, collies, schnauzers and cocker spaniels are more examples of long-haired dogs.

Try painting a whole basketful of fluffy pups.

This "pocket pet" sized portrait of a German shepherd would make a great paperweight.

Other Ideas

Here's a portrait of a wire-haired terrier.

Whether or not they get along in real life, you can always paint a loving family portrait of your pets.

You couldn't help but take these little orphans if left on your doorstep.

Index